CONTRIBUTORS

Ray L. Birdwhistell
Edmund Carpenter
H. J. Chaytor
Lawrence K. Frank
Northrop Frye
Arthur Gibson
S. Giedion
Stephen Gilman
Robert Graves
Stanley Edgar Hyman

Dorothy Lee
Fernand Léger
Marshall McLuhan
David Riesman
W. R. Rodgers
Gilbert Seldes
Jean Shepherd
Daisetz T. Suzuki
Jacqueline Tyrwhitt

EXPLORATIONS
IN COMMUNICATION

An Anthology

Edited by Edmund Carpenter and Marshall McLuhan

Beacon Press   Boston

ACKNOWLEDGMENTS

All the essays in this anthology appeared in *Explorations,* a journal published at the University of Toronto under a Ford Foundation grant. A few had appeared earlier, usually in different form; a few, first printed in *Explorations* were later reprinted elsewhere.

With two exceptions, all the essays are reprinted in this anthology with the permission of the authors. ("Pure Color" by Fernand Léger was given to Jacqueline Tyrwhitt by the author and subsequently translated by her when she was an editor of *Explorations.* "Joyce's Wake" by W. R. Rodgers is taken from the tape of a BBC radio program, "The Portrait of James Joyce," which was edited by Mr. Rodgers and produced by Maurice Brown.)

The editors wish to thank each author represented in this anthology, as well as the following publishers and copyright holders, for permission to use material under their control:

AMERICAN ANTHROPOLOGICAL ASSOCIATION for short excerpts from *Autobiography of a Papago Woman* by Ruth Underhill, 1936.

APPLETON-CENTURY-CROFTS, INC. for short excerpts from *American English Grammar* by Charles C. Fries, copyright, 1940, The National Council of Teachers of English and Charles C. Fries.

DENIS DOBSON, LTD. for short excerpts from *Theory of Film* by Béla Balázs, 1953.

FABER AND FABER, LTD. for a short excerpt from *Film of Murder in the Cathedral* by George Hoellering and T. S. Eliot, 1952.

S. GIEDION for his article "Space Conception in Prehistoric Art," which was delivered as a Mellon Lecture, National Gallery, Washington, 1957, and will serve as a chapter in *Constancy and Change in Early Art and Architecture,* a forthcoming Bollingen Foundation publication.

HARCOURT, BRACE & CO. for a short excerpt from *Film of Murder in the Cathedral* by George Hoellering and T. S. Eliot, 1952.

HARPER & BROTHERS for "Buddhist Symbolism" by Daisetz T. Suzuki, which appeared in their book *Symbols and Values: An Initial Study,* 13th Symposium of the Conference on Science, Philosophy and Religion, edited by Lyman Bryson *et al.,* 1955.

HARVARD UNIVERSITY PRESS for a short excerpt from *Public Opinion in Russia* by Alex Inkeles, 1950.

W. HEFFER AND SONS, LTD. for "Reading and Writing" by H. J. Chaytor, which appeared in their book *From Script to Print*, 1950.

PAUL B. HOEBER, INC. for "Lineal and Nonlineal Codifications of Reality" by Dorothy Lee, which appeared in their publication *Psychosomatic Medicine*, no. 12, May 1950.

INTERNATIONAL JOURNAL OF AMERICAN LINGUISTICS for "Linguistic Reflection of Wintu Thought" by Dorothy Lee, which appeared in the Vol. 10, 1944 issue.

ELIA KAZAN and NEWTOWN PRODUCTIONS, INC. for a short excerpt from "Writers and Motion Pictures." This article appeared in *The Atlantic Monthly*, 199, 1957.

EDMUND MORGAN for a short excerpt from *The Legacy of Sacco and Vanzetti* by G. Louis Joughin and Edmund M. Morgan, Harcourt, Brace & Co., 1948.

THOMAS NELSON AND SONS, LTD. for a short excerpt from *Our Spoken Language* by A. Lloyd Jones, 1938.

PRENTICE-HALL, INC. for "Lineal and Nonlineal Codifications of Reality" and "Linguistic Reflection of Wintu Thought" by Dorothy Lee, both of which appeared in their book *Freedom and Culture*, 1959.

PRINCETON UNIVERSITY PRESS for "The Language of Poetry" by Northrop Frye, which appeared in their book *Anatomy of Criticism*, 1957.

ROY PUBLISHERS for short excerpts from *Theory of Film* by Béla Balázs, 1953.

MARTIN SECKER & WARBURG, LTD. for short excerpts from *Voices of Silence* by André Malraux, 1954.

RUTH UNDERHILL for short excerpts from *Autobiography of a Papago Woman*, American Anthropological Association, 1936.

WILLIS KINGSLEY WING for "Comments on 'Lineal and Nonlineal Codifications of Reality'" by Robert Graves.

YALE UNIVERSITY PRESS for short excerpts from *On Principles and Methods in Latin Syntax* by Edward P. Morris, Charles Scribner's Sons, 1902.

CONTENTS

INTRODUCTION

The articles in this anthology come from *Explorations*, a journal on communications published between 1953 and 1959. All its issues are now rare collectors' items.

Explorations explored the grammars of such languages as print, the newspaper format and television. It argued that revolutions in the packaging and distribution of ideas and feelings modified not only human relations but also sensibilities. It further argued that we are largely ignorant of literacy's role in shaping Western man, and equally unaware of the role of electronic media in shaping modern values. Literacy's vested interests were so deep that literacy itself was never examined. And the current electronic revolution is already so pervasive that we have difficulty in stepping outside of it and scrutinizing it objectively. But it can be done, and a fruitful approach is to examine one medium through another: print seen from the perspective of electronic media, or television analyzed through print.

De Tocqueville, to study democracy, went to the New World, for he realized that colonial America had a huge advantage over Europe. It was able to develop and apply swiftly all the consequences of printing (in the book, the newspaper and, by extension, the assembly line in industry and organization) because there was no backlog of obsolete technology to be liquidated first. Europeans had to struggle through a long, painful period in order to clear enough room to exploit the new print technology.

Today America has the largest backlog of obsolete technology in the world: its educational and industrial establishments, built by print and methods derived from print, are vast and pervasive. Backward countries have a huge advantage over us: they now stand in relation to electronic technology much as we once stood in relation to print technology. What we plan to do or can do to brainwash ourselves of this obsolete inheritance has yet to be faced.

The relevant factor in this obsolescence is the use of electronic tapes by which information is fed from several points simultaneously and in concert; previously, with print, there had been one unit followed by another unit. With this switch from linear to cluster configuration, literacy lost its main prop in the social structure of our time, because the motivating force in the teaching of reading, and the development of a highly literate culture, was the strict relevance of that classroom discipline to every pattern and purpose in the outside world. Today the outside world is abandoning that very form and providing increasingly less motivation for the teaching of reading and the achieving of literate culture in our schools.

Our very concepts of media analysis are literary, limited to content analysis and unrelated to the new configurations of electronic media. Probably the best way to analyze media is through "organized ignorance." This striking phrase seems to have arisen during the Second World War, when the Operations Research people put biologists and psychologists to work on weapons problems that would ordinarily have fallen to the lot of engineers and physicists. The former group swarmed all over each problem instead of beaming a ray of specialized knowledge at it. If you beam knowledge at a new situation, you find it is quite opaque; if you organize your ignorance, tackling the situation as an over-all project, probing all aspects at the same time, you find unexpected apertures, vistas, breakthroughs. Thus the chemist Mendeleev, to discover the missing group in the element chart, did not simply use available knowledge. Instead he asked: what must be the characteristics of the rest, if those we do know are to make sense among themselves?

Rouault formulated "light-through, rather than light-on" by painting stained glass. The peculiarity of television, as distinguished from photographs and movies, is that the image is constituted by light-through; shifting mosaic illuminations project themselves at the viewer. The light-through mode of communication, calling for total illumination from within, is strikingly different from the analytic modes of literacy, which create a habit of perception and analysis that deliberately, and by organized means, ignores all but one thing at a time.

The phonetic alphabet and all its derivatives stress a one-thing-at-a-time analytic awareness in perception. This intensity of analysis is achieved at the price of forcing all else in the field of perception into the subliminal. For 2500 years we have lived in what Joyce called "ABCED-mindedness." We win, as a result of this fragmenting of the field of perception and the breaking of movement into static bits, a power of applied knowledge and technology unrivaled in human history. The price we pay is existing personally and socially in a state of almost total subliminal awareness.

In the present age of all-at-onceness, we have discovered that it is impossible—personally, collectively, technologically—to live with the subliminal. Paradoxically, at this moment in our culture, we meet once more preliterate man. For him there was no subliminal factor in experience; his mythic forms of explanation explicated all levels of any situation at the same time. This is why Freud makes no sense when applied to pre- and postliterate man.

Postliterate man's electronic media contract the world to a village or tribe where everything happens to everyone at the same time: everyone knows about, and therefore participates in, everything that is happening the minute it happens. Television gives this quality of simultaneity to events in the global village.

This simultaneous sharing of experiences as in a village or tribe creates a village or tribal outlook, and puts a premium on togetherness. In this new tribal juxtaposition of people, nobody strives for individual excellence, which would be socially suicidal and is therefore taboo. Teen-agers deliberately seek mediocrity as a means of achieving togetherness. They are strengthened in this tendency by the goading of the adult world, which is essentially individualistic. Teen-agers want to be artists, but they cannot stay "together" if they are exceptional; therefore they boycott the exceptional.

Just as the Eskimo has been de-tribalized via print, going in the course of a few years from primitive nomad to literate technician, so we, in an equally brief period, are becoming tribalized via electronic channels. The literacy we abandon, he embraces; the oral language he rejects, we accept. Whether this is good or bad remains to be seen. At the moment, it is important that we understand cause and process. The aim of this anthology is to develop an awareness about print and the newer technologies of communication so that we can orchestrate them, minimize their mutual frustrations and clashes, and get the best out of each in the educational process. The present conflict leads to elimination of the motive to learn and to diminution of interest in all previous achievement: it leads to loss of the sense of relevance. Without an understanding of media grammars, we cannot hope to achieve a contemporary awareness of the world in which we live.

EXPLORATIONS IN COMMUNICATION

CLASSROOM WITHOUT WALLS

Marshall McLuhan

It's natural today to speak of "audio-visual aids" to teaching, for we still think of the book as norm, of other media as incidental. We also think of the new media (press, radio, TV) as *mass media* and think of the book as an individualistic form —individualistic because it isolated the reader in silence and helped create the Western "I." Yet it was the first product of mass production.

With it everybody could have the same books. It was impossible in medieval times for different students, different institutions, to have copies of the same book. Manuscripts, commentaries, were dictated. Students memorized. Instruction was almost entirely oral, done in groups. Solitary study was reserved for the advanced scholar. The first printed books were "visual aids" to oral instruction.

Before the printing press, the young learned by listening, watching, doing. So, until recently, our own rural children learned the language and skills of their elders. Learning took place outside the classroom. Only those aiming at professional careers went to school at all. Today in our cities, most learning occurs outside the classroom. The sheer quantity of information conveyed by press-magazines-film-TV-radio far exceeds the quantity of information conveyed by school instruction and texts. This challenge has destroyed the monopoly of the book as a teaching aid and cracked the very walls of the classroom so suddenly that we're confused, baffled.

In this violently upsetting social situation, many teachers naturally view the offerings of the new media as entertainment, rather than education. But this carries no conviction to the student. Find a classic that wasn't first regarded as light entertain-

ment. Nearly all vernacular works were so regarded until the
19th century.

Many movies are obviously handled with a degree of insight
and maturity at least equal to the level permitted in today's textbooks. Olivier's *Henry V* and *Richard III* assemble a wealth of
scholarly and artistic skill, which reveals Shakespeare at a very
high level, yet in a way easy for the young to enjoy.

The movie is to dramatic representation what the book was
to the manuscript. It makes available to many and at many times
and places what otherwise would be restricted to a few at few
times and places. The movie, like the book, is a ditto device.
TV shows to 50,000,000 simultaneously. Some feel that the value
of experiencing a book is diminished by being extended to many
minds. This notion is always implicit in the phrases "mass media,"
"mass entertainment"—useless phrases obscuring the fact that
English itself is a mass medium.

Today we're beginning to realize that the new media aren't
just mechanical gimmicks for creating worlds of illusion, but new
languages with new and unique powers of expression. Histori-
cally, the resources of English have been shaped and expressed
in constantly new and changing ways. The printing press changed
not only the quantity of writing but also the character of language and the relations between author and public. Radio, film,
TV pushed written English toward the spontaneous shifts and
freedom of the spoken idiom. They aided us in the recovery of
intense awareness of facial language and bodily gesture. If these
"mass media" should serve only to weaken or corrupt previously
achieved levels of verbal and pictorial culture, it won't be because
there's anything inherently wrong with them. It will be because
we've failed to master them as new languages in time to assimilate them to our total cultural heritage.

These new developments, under quiet analytic survey, point
to a basic strategy of culture for the classroom. When the printed
book first appeared, it threatened the oral procedures of teaching and created the classroom as we now know it. Instead of
making his own text, his own dictionary, his own grammar, the
student started out with these tools. He could study not one but
several languages. Today these new media threaten, instead of

merely reinforce, the procedures of this traditional classroom. It's customary to answer this threat with denunciations of the unfortunate character and effect of movies and TV, just as the comic book was feared and scorned and rejected from the classroom. Its good and bad features in form and content, when carefully set beside other kinds of art and narrative, could have become a major asset to the teacher.

Where student interest is already focused is the natural point at which to be in the elucidation of other problems and interests. The educational task is not only to provide basic tools of perception but also to develop judgment and discrimination with ordinary social experience.

Few students ever acquire skill in analysis of newspapers. Fewer have any ability to discuss a movie intelligently. To be articulate and discriminating about ordinary affairs and information is the mark of an educated man. It's misleading to suppose there's any basic difference between education and entertainment. This distinction merely relieves people of the responsibility of looking into the matter. It's like setting up a distinction between didactic and lyric poetry on the ground that one teaches, the other pleases. However, it's always been true that whatever pleases teaches more effectively.

TACTILE COMMUNICATION

Lawrence K. Frank

I recently heard of a man who bought a pet armadillo. Before taking it home, he sprayed it under its plates, again and again, with DDT: insects fell until they darkened the floor. But within days the armadillo sickened. The owner was advised to put parasites back under the plates, a remedy that proved successful. I believe a major problem was involved here.

The skin serves both as receptor and transmitter of messages, some of which are culturally defined. Its acute sensitivity allows the development of such an elaborate system as Braille, but tactilism is more basic than such oddities imply and constitutes a fundamental communication form.

In infancy there is recognition and response first to *signals*, then to *signs*, finally to *symbols*. The infant arrives with a repertory of biological signals; he responds to these in patterns of reflexes such as coughing, yawning, sneezing, and swallowing. When two signals are received more or less concomitantly, as in a conditioned reflex experiment, the second, so-called unconditioned and previously indifferent signal, may become the surrogate or sign for the first. Still later the infant learns that not only are these signs defined by others but their responses are defined as well. And thus he begins to use culturally patterned tactile symbols.

In time this early form of communication is augmented by speech; in part it may lay the foundation for learning speech. The mother will console her infant by patting him, later by both pats and words, and finally, from the other room, "It's all right, Johnny. I'm right here."

Tactile communication is never wholly superseded; it is merely elaborated by the symbolic process. Cassirer remarks,

4

"Vocal language has a very great technical advantage over tactile language; but the technical defects of the latter do not destroy its essential use." In some interpersonal relations it communicates more fully than speech, e.g., consoling a bereaved person, when "words fail." In *After Many a Summer Dies the Swan,* Huxley writes, "The direct animal intuitions aren't rendered by words; the words merely remind you of your memories of similar experience." I may say I have an intuitive *feeling*, that it was a *touching* experience, and thus refer to an earlier and perhaps more basic medium than language itself.

The Skin

Tactual sensitivity is probably the most primitive sensory process, appearing as tropism or thigmotaxis in the lowest organism. Many infrahuman organisms orient themselves by feelers or antennae by which they *feel* their way through life. It is also of major importance in human life.

The human skin, with only vestigial body hair, is probably more sensitive than that of other mammals, although movement of the hair can stimulate cutaneous sensations by follicular displacements: stroking "against the grain" may tickle, "with the grain" may prove soothing. Petting the baby rhythmically not only soothes him but apparently promotes his well-being and metabolic efficiency. Caressing, also rhythmic, is of immense significance in adult life.

Rats that have been gentled are better able to metabolize food and are less susceptible to various forms of shock, experimentally produced convulsions, and so on. Those raised from birth with a cardboard ruff around their necks to prevent them from licking their own bodies are unable to care for their young by licking them. Kittens cannot urinate or defecate unless the mother licks the anus or urethra and thereby elicits evacuation.

Orbelli found what he called "sympathetic connections" from the skin to the smooth muscle of the intestines that provide pathways for the conduction of soothing, licking stimulation to these highly motile organs. The gut, from mouth to anus, is lined with epithelial cells not unrelated to the skin and derived from the same embryological layer. Moreover, the end organs for tactile stimuli are richly provided in and around the mouth and anus, and in the genitals, and are numerous or sensitive in the skin adjacent to these parts. Orbelli's findings have not been confirmed; yet it is difficult to see how tactile soothing operates unless there are other modes of conduction than the presently recognized sensory processes of warm-cold, pain, and pressure.

We can say that the skin, as a communication organ, is highly complex and versatile, with an immense range of functional operations and a wide repertory of responses. These can only be understood by assuming a more richly endowed sensory-nervous system than the warm-cold-pain-pressure categories: probably the sympathetic innervation of the sweat glands and capillaries is conductive to the viscera and perhaps to other organ systems. Insofar as capillary dilation and constriction by cold or warmth either initiate or accelerate alterations in the circulation of the blood, tactile stimulation—especially rhythmic caressing—may prove a major component of the homeostatic process. A person in fear or pain may recover his physiological equilibrium through tactual contacts with a sympathetic person.

Bott once showed that the third finger was passively the most sensitive to a hair esthesiometer, while the forefinger was much more sensitive when used purposefully to detect a hair concealed under a cigarette paper. In other words, an individual has a selective, variable tactile awareness, not unrelated to purposive conduct.

Personality Development

Tactual sensitivity appears early in fetal life as probably the first sensory process to become functional. The fetus more or less floats in the amniotic fluid and continuously receives the rhythmic impacts of the maternal heart beat, impinging on the skin of his whole body and magnified by the fluid. His own heart beat will later synchronize or be out of tune with the maternal heart beat; in either case he experiences a series of impacts upon his skin to which he develops a continuous response, as a physiological resonance. Thus, even before birth he adjusts to a rhythmically pulsating environment. At birth he experiences pressures and constrictions, which are sometimes intense, and then suddenly he is exposed to atmospheric pressures and an altered temperature, which evoke respiratory activity and presumably a number of tactile responses.

The newborn mammal "needs" to be nuzzled, cuddled, and licked by its mother; it remains close to her body, receiving warmth and close tactual contacts, plus frequent licking and nursing. The treatment of the human infant may conform to this pattern or depart drastically from it. Some infants are kept close to the mother, may be given the colostrum, allowed to nurse freely and as long as desired; others may have such tactile contacts sharply curtailed. But in most instances the child is nuzzled and licked and patted rhythmically; he touches his lips to his mother's body, more specifically to the nipple, and increasingly fingers her body. By such means he evokes from her the stimulation that he "needs": warmth, milk, and so on.

It seems probable that the newborn infant, with its undeveloped, inadequate capacity for homeostasis, requires these experiences for maintenance of his internal equilibrium. Thus, he keeps warm through bodily contacts; he maintains, or recovers, his equilibrium when disturbed by fear, pain, hunger, or cold through rhythmic tactual stimulation like patting, stroking, caressing. The emotionally disturbed infant usually responds with increasing composure to patting or even vigorous, but rhythmic, slapping on the back. What might awaken or keep awake an older child, puts an infant to sleep; this age difference supports the assumption of an early infantile sensitivity or need for rhythmic tactual stimulation that fades out or is incorporated into other patterns.

The baby begins to communicate with himself by feeling his own body, exploring its shape and textures, and thereby to establish his body image. Later he focuses his vision upon his feet and fingers and so begins to build up visual images to reinforce tactile experiences.

The quality or intent of the message, as contrasted with its content, may be conveyed by the emotional coloring-tone of voice, facial expression, gesture, or lightness of touch, and the recipient responds largely to this intent or quality. Usually the mother speaks or hums or sings to the child as she pats or cuddles him, and thus he learns to recognize the sound of her voice as a surrogate for her touch. In time her reassuring words are accepted as equivalents of tactile experience, even though she isn't within touching distance. Equally, he may learn to recognize a note of displeasure in her voice and may cringe, as if to physical punishment that he has experienced previously when scolded. It seems clear that his reception of verbal messages is predicated in large measure upon his prior tactile experience.

The baby's initial spatial orientation occurs through tactile explorations: feeling with hands and often with the lips, and testing out the quality, size, shape, texture, and density of whatever he can reach. These manipulations involve motor activities and increasingly skillful neuromuscular coordinations, established through tactile messages and gradually replaced by visual cues. Bumps, pain, warmth are primary tactile signals; visual signs— size, shape, appearance, color—later become their surrogates. It is often forgotten how much prolonged learning was required to master these motor patterns. The adult rarely recalls how, in early life, he relied upon touch for his initial orientation to the spatial dimensions of the world.

Thus the baby's perception of the world is built upon and shaped by tactile experiences. These become increasingly overlaid by other symbolic patterns, so much so that they often become inaccessible, except through such experiences as finger painting, clay-modeling, water play. Perhaps the potency of music and poetry, with their rhythmical patterning and varying intensities of sounds, depends in large measure upon the provision of an auditory surrogate for primary tactile experiences.

The child begins by exploring everything within reach, but gradually he learns that there are prohibitions involving both people and things, and he begins to curtail his contacts. He is taught to impute inviolability to what was previously accessible, and thereby is inducted into the social world with its elaborate codes of respect for property and persons.

Moreover, the child learns to distinguish, first by tactile means, between the "me" and the "not-me." Later he modifies these definitions, casting them largely in verbal form, but the tactile definitions nevertheless remain prior and basic.

Babies seem to differ widely in their need for tactile experiences and in their response to such ministrations. Deprivation of such experiences may compromise the infant's future learning, particularly of speech and, indeed, of all symbolic systems, including more mature tactile communication. If severely limited in these experiences, presumably he must wait until his capacities for visual and auditory communication are developed sufficiently to permit him to enter into satisfactory communication with others.

Such a child may become unusually dependent upon the authority of his parents and overly obedient to their pronouncements; he will lack the experience of prior communication, and he may find the sudden jump not only difficult but conducive to unhealthy relationships. Perhaps this offers clues to schizophrenic personalities who are unable to enter fully and effectively into the symbolic world of others and many of whom are reported to be rejected babies, deprived of mothering. It may also throw light upon the impairment of abstract thinking observed in children separated from their mothers. There is evidence as well that not only reading disabilities but also speech retardation and difficulties arise from early deprivation of, and confusion in, tactile communication. Such deprivation may evoke exploratory searches for surrogates: masturbation, thumb sucking, fingering the nose, ears, hair, or reliance on other modes of communication.

The child is often alienated from his mother around five or six, when this seeking and giving tactual contacts begin to diminish in our culture. We see boys evading or being denied such contacts, although with girls it may continue longer. This diminution of tactual sensitivity and experiences, characteristic of middle childhood, the so-called latency period, ceases abruptly at puberty when the boy and girl become avid for such contacts, seeking to touch and be touched. In adolescence, tactile communication increases, at first between members of the same sex, as boys walk together with arms on each other's shoulders, girls with arms around each other's waists, and then with the first tentative heterosexual explorations. Tactile communication in adult mating has been elaborated by some cultures into extremely complex patterns.

Cultural Patterning

Each culture activates or limits tactile communication, not only between its members, but between the individual and his outer world, for at every moment man is communicating with his environment, receiving and responding to stimuli, often without conscious awareness (e.g., pressure on feet or buttocks, cool breezes, smoking).

Skin color can serve as a visual identification, eliciting responses that are often tactile, e.g., avoiding contacts, the desire to touch. The amount of clothing and the parts of the body covered differ by culture and according to time, place, and occasion. The body arts, including painting, tattooing, incising, and the use of cosmetics generally, are ways of enhancing the skin's appearance, just as grooming the skin, especially mutual grooming, bathing, anointing, perfuming, and shaving are patterns for modifying the skin to indicate tactual readiness for communication. Thus body arts and grooming serve as surrogates for invitations to tactile contacts, real or symbolic; the "admiring glance" indicates that the message was received, understood, and accepted.

Such decorations are of significance in the performance of roles and allow others to respond appropriately. In large part the masculine and feminine roles are defined by patterns of skin exposure, body arts, clothing, and the kinds of tactile contacts permitted between them. Every culture has a well-established code for such communications. Shame, blushing, and pallor may be associated with their violation; modesty, with their observance.

Tactile communication is of importance in the establishment of the inviolability of things and persons under penalties for unsanctioned approach. Indeed, the incest taboo itself, so basic to social organization, is learned primarily in terms of tactile restrictions. The "don't touch" extends as well to material objects and involves a wide array of property rights; the infant's first eager explorations are channeled, and soon he learns not only *who* but *whose*. Gradually he transforms these parental prohibitions into self-administered inhibitions by learning to perceive things and persons as signs or symbols for avoidance.

It may be safe to say that much of a kinship system, as well as rank, caste, role, age, is learned and maintained in terms of touch. The handshake, with removal of glove, close dancing, rubbing noses, kissing, the arm around the shoulder or waist— all these are sharply defined, as are the tactile experiences of love-making. The texture of food, the "feel" of a fabric, the temperature of a drink, are defined both culturally and personally. Manufacturers report difficulty in marketing products that meet all requirements save that of "feeling right": metal furniture feels too cold, plastic dinnerware too light. We even judge a painting, not only on form, colors, and content, but also by texture, by how it would feel if we touched it. Perhaps our appreciation of sculpture is reduced by the art gallery sign: "Do Not Touch."

Communication with the self by masturbation is probably universal, but sanctioned by only some cultures. Other forms of tactile communication with the self are tics, scratching, patting the hair, pressing against objects, and massage, the last also being the focus of professional practices. Finally, each culture sets patterns of painful experiences that must be accepted: spanking, slapping the face, fire walking or handling, scarification, stoical acceptance of cold or wounds.

Highly abstract concepts seem to lie outside the range of most tactile messages and probably occur only in such a system as Braille.

LINGUISTIC REFLECTION OF WINTU THOUGHT

Dorothy Lee

The study presented below was made on the assumption that the language of a society is one of the symbolic systems in which the structured world-view is expressed. According to this assumption systems of kinship, ritual, and other aspects of cultural symbolization and behavior will yield, upon analysis, the same basis for conceptualization and categorization, the same approach to reality and definition of truth.

A basic tenet of the Wintu language, expressed in both nominal and verbal categories, is that reality—ultimate truth—exists irrespective of man. Man's experience actualizes this reality but does not otherwise affect its being. Outside man's experience, this reality is unbounded, undifferentiated, timeless. Man believes it but does not know it. He refers to it in his speech but does not assert it; he leaves it untouched by his senses, inviolate. Within his experience, the reality assumes temporality and limits. As it impinges upon his consciousness he imposes temporary shape upon it. Out of the undifferentiated qualities and essences of the given reality, he individuates and particularizes, impressing himself diffidently and transiently, performing acts of will with circumspection. Matter and relationships, essence, quality are all given. The Wintu actualizes a given design, endowing it with temporality and form through his experience. But he neither creates nor changes; the design remains immutable.

The given as undifferentiated content is implicit in the nominal categories of the Wintu. Nouns—except for kinship terms, which are classified with pronouns—all make reference primarily to generic substance. To the Wintu, the given is not a series of particulars, to be classed into universals. The given is unpartitioned mass; a part of this the Wintu delimits into a particular individual. The particular then exists, not in nature, but in the consciousness of the speaker. What to us is a class, a plurality of particulars, is to him a mass or a quality or an attribute. These concepts are one for the Wintu; the word for *red*, for example, is the same as for *redness* or *red-mass*. Plurality, on the other hand, is not derived from the singular and is of slight interest to him. He has no nominal plural form, and when he does use a plural word, such as *men*, he uses a root that is completely different from the singular word; *man* is wi'Da but *men* is q'i·s.

To someone brought up in the Indo-European tradition, this is a position hard to understand. We know that the plural is derived from the singular. It is logical and natural for our grammars to start with the singular form of a noun or a verb and then go on to the plural. When we are faced with words like *group* or *herd* or *flock*, we call them, as a matter of course, collective plurals. Words like *sheep* or *deer*, which make no morphological distinction between singular and plural, are explained on the basis of historical accident or the mechanics of enunciation. But to the Wintu it is natural to speak of deer or salmon without distinction of number; to him a flock is a whole, not a collection of singular individuals. To us, the distinction of number is so important that we cannot mention an object unless we also simultaneously indicate whether it is singular or plural; and if we speak of it in the present tense, the verb we use must echo this number. And the Greek had to do more than this; if he had to make a statement such as *the third man who entered was old and blind*, the words *third, who entered, was, old,* and *blind,* though referring to nonquantitative concepts, all had to reiterate the singularity of the man. The Wintu, on the other hand, indicates number only if he, the speaker, chooses to do so. In such a case he can qualify his noun with a word such as *many* or *one*; or he can express plurality of object or subject through special forms of the verb.

The care that we bestow on the distinction of number is lavished by the Wintu on the distinction between particular and generic. But here is a further difference. Whereas we find num-

ber already present in substance itself, the Wintu imposes par-
ticularity upon substance. We *must* use a plural when we are
confronted by plural objects; the Wintu *chooses* to use a partic-
ularizing form. It is true that for certain nouns, such as those
referring to live people and animals, the Wintu uses a particular-
izing form almost always; that for substances that we, also, regard
as generic, such as fire and sand and wood, he almost always uses
a generic form. But these are merely habitual modes of speaking from which he can and does deviate.

His distinction, then, is subjective. He starts from *whiteness*
or *white* (χayi), a quality, and derives from this, as an observer,
the particular—the *white one* (χayit). With the use of derivative suffixes, he delimits a part of the mass. We take the word
for *deer* (no·B+'; the ' is the sign of the particular in the nominative), for example. In the instances I give, I shall use only the
objective case, no·B for the generic, and no·Bum for the particular. A hunter went out but saw no *deer*, no·B; another killed a
deer, no·Bum. A woman carried *deer*, no·B, to her mother; a
hunter brought home *deer*, no·Bum. Now the woman's deer was
cut in pieces and carried, a formless mass, in her back-basket; but
the man carried his two deer slung whole from his shoulder.
Some brothers were about to eat venison; they called, "Old man,
come and eat *venison*, (no·B)." The old man replied, "You can
eat that stinking *venison*, (no·Bum) yourselves." The brothers
saw it just as deer-meat; to the old man it was the flesh of a particular deer, one that had been killed near human habitation, fed
on human offal. I have recorded two versions of the same tale,
told respectively by a man and a woman. The man refers to a
man's weapons and implements in the particular; the woman men-
tions them all as generic. The use of the word sem (seᶜ) is illu-
minating in this connection. As generic, sem, it means *hand* or
both hands of one person, the fingers merged in one mass; spread
out the hand, and now you have delimited parts of the hand,
semum, *fingers*.

For the Wintu, then, essence, or quality, is generic and found
in nature; it is permanent and remains unaffected by man. Form
is imposed by man, through act of will. But the impress man

makes is temporary. The deer stands out as an individual only at the moment of his speech; as soon as he ceases speaking, the deer merges into deerness.

The concept of the immutability of essence and the transiency of form, of the fleeting significance of delimitation, is reflected in Wintu mythology. Matter was always there; the creator, *He who is above*, a vague being, was really a Former. People do not *come into being*, as I say in my faulty literal translation of the myths; they *grow out of the ground*; they always existed. Dawn and daylight, fire and obsidian have always been in existence, hoarded; they are finally stolen, and give a new role. In the myths, various characters *form* men out of materials that are already present; Coyote, for example, changes sticks into men. Throughout, form is shifting and relatively unimportant. The characters, Coyote, Buzzard, Grizzly Bear, etc., are bewilderingly men and animals in their attributes, never assuming stable form. Even this semi-defined form may be changed with ease; Grosbeak is steamed faultily, for example, and turns into a grasshopper. The Wintu speak of these characters in English as *Coyote, Loon*, not *a coyote*. We have assumed that by this they mean a proper name. But it is probable that they refer to something undelimited, as we, for example, distinguish between fire and a fire. These characters die and reappear in another myth without explanation. They become eventually the coyotes and grizzly bears we know, but not through a process of generation. They represent a prototype, a genus, a quality that, however, is not rigidly differentiated from other qualities.

The premise of primacy of the whole finds expression in the Wintu concept of himself as originally one, not a sum of limbs or members. When I asked for a word for the body, I was given the term *the whole person*. The Wintu does not say *my head aches*; he says *I head ache*. He does not say *my hands are hot;* he says *I hands am hot*. He does not say *my leg*, except extremely rarely and for good reason, such as that his leg has been severed from his body. The clothes he wears are part of this whole. A Wintu girl does not say *her dress was striped* but *she was-dress-striped*. In dealing with the whole, the various aspects referred to are generic; only when particularization is necessary as a device to distinguish toes or fingers from feet and hands is it used. But when the leg is not part of the whole, when the subject is cutting out the heart of a victim, then particularization is used, since the activity is seen from the point of view of the subject. And when a woman is ironing her dress, which is not part of her body any more, she refers to it as something separate: *my dress*.

In his verbal phrase, the Wintu shows himself again humble in the face of immutable reality, but not paralyzed into inactivity. Here again he is faced with being that is, irrespective of himself, and that he must accept without question. A limited part of this comes within his ken; his consciousness, cognition, and sensation act as a limiting and formalizing element upon the formless reality. Of this delimited part he speaks completely in terms of the bounds of his own person. He uses a stem, derived from the primary root, which means *I know*, or *this is within experience*. The definitive suffixes that he uses with this convey, in every case, the particular source of his information, or, to put it differently, the particular aspect of himself through which he has become cognizant of what he states. The material he presents has become known to him through his eyes—"the child is playing (-be) in the sand"; or through his other senses—"this is sour (-nte)" or "he is yelling (-nte)"; or through his logic—"he is hungry (-el; he must be hungry since he has had no food for two days)"; or through the action of logic upon the circumstantial evidence of the senses—"a doe went by with two fawns (-re; I see their tracks)"; or through his acceptance of hearsay evidence —"they fought long (-ke; someone told me)." In this category of experience, the future is stated in terms of intention or desire or attempt. This is a future that depends on an act of will and is not stated with certainty. This is the aspect of experience with which the unreflective among us concern themselves exclusively; as one of my students asked: "And what is left outside?"

Outside is the reality that is beyond personal cognition, a reality that is accepted in faith. For this, the Wintu uses the primary form of the verb. Alone, this stem forms a command; yoqu means *wash! you must wash*, a reference to given necessity. With the aid of different suffixes, this stem may refer to a timeless state, as when setting given conditions for a certain activity, or to what we call the passive, when the individual does not participate as a free agent. In general, it refers to the not-experienced and not-known. To this stem is appended the nonassertive -mina, and the resulting verbal form contains, then, potentially both positive and negative alternatives simultaneously. With the proper auxiliaries, this may be used either to negate, or to ask a question requiring a yes-or-no answer, or in phrases implying ignorance; but it can never assert the known. And when a Wintu gives a negative command, he uses this form again; he does not say "don't chop" but *may it remain unactualized-chop* (k'oBmina). To this not-experienced, timeless, necessary reality, the Wintu refers chiefly in terms of natural necessity; by means of one suffix, -le's (a nominal form of -le), he refers to a future that must be realized, to a probability that is at the same time potential, necessary, and inevitable. Words modified by this suffix are translated by the Wintu variously with the aid of *may,* or *might,* or *would,* or *must,* or *can* or *shall.* Another reference to this reality is made with the aid of the unmodified -le. This suffix can be used with personal suffixes, to indicate a future of certainty, in the realization of which the subject does not participate as a free agent. It is a future so certain that this form, also, is sometimes translated with *must:* for example, "You, too, shall die." Without personal endings, the -le ties together two events or states of being in inevitable sequence, with no reference to specific time. The sequence may be translated by the Wintu with the aid of the purposive *so as to,* or *to* or with *about to,* but there is no subjective purpose involved; or the word *before* may be used in the translation. Now, the -le refers to a succession of events in nature and to an inevitable sequence. But here the Wintu can act of his own free will and decide on one of the members of the sequence. He can interpolate an act of choice and thus bring about a desired sequence. Or the subject can intercept an undesirable sequence, by changing the first unit. The same stem is used for this, but the Wintu add a different suffix, -ken (second person), which they translate as either *so that you should not* or *you might*

or *don't;* that is, the suffix warns of the pending sequence and
implies: avoid it. For example, a man shouts to his daughter who
is standing on a ladder, *Be careful, you might fall off* or *don't fall
off* (talken). Some one instructs two boys: sight carefully when
you shoot, *so as not to miss,* or *you might miss,* or *don't miss*
(manaken). And a woman who hears that a rattlesnake has been
seen near the water says, "Let me not go swimming; I *might get
stung* (t'optcukida)." Bia ihkedi: *he might do it himself,* or *don't
let him do it,* is, according to my informant, equivalent to saying,
"You'd better do it yourself." So the role of the Wintu in the future is not creative but can be formative; i.e., it may be negative,
or it may take the form of an interpolation between necessary
events. Here, again, the act of will exists but appears as restrained and limited.

It is impossible to tell to what extent the reluctance to penetrate beyond external form is active in the formation of words.
If the Wintu offers me an English word in translation for a Wintu
one, I rarely have any way of knowing what exactly the word
means to him. When he says that watca· is *to weep,* for example,
is he, like me, thinking of the whole kinesthetic activity with all
its emotional implications, or is he merely concerned with the
sound of weeping, as I think he is? Whenever I find a group of
words derived from the same root, I can clearly see that they
point to a preoccupation with form alone. I find in my glossary
a word for *to shave the head* (poyoqDe·luna·), for example.
There is no reason to question the English rendering till I examine the root from which it is derived. I find other derivatives
from this root. One means *to pull off a scab;* another, *to have a
damp forehead.* If there is to be a common meaning the first is
not concerned with the activity of prying off a scab or with the
sensation of the skin; it refers only to the glistening skin exposed.
Neither is the second concerned with the sensation of dampness,
but, again, merely with the appearance of the skin. So, though
the Wintu uses *to shave the head* as equivalent to poyoqDe·luna·,
I am concerned, rather, with the activity of cutting itself, with
the feel of the scalp, the complete removal of hair, whereas the
Wintu refers only to the way the end result appears to the ob-

server; his word means *to make one's own scalp glisten*. I have
recorded a word that applies to the pounding of non-brittle objects. I have translated it as *to pound to a pulp*. I have passed
judgment as to what happens to the consistency of the buckeye
when I pound it. But the Wintu is merely making a statement
as to the external form of the pounded mass; from this word
Dira·, he derives his word for De·rus, *tick*.

The same insistence upon outward form alone has influenced
the naming of White traits. Where I say *he plays the piano*, the
Wintu says *he makes a braying noise*. I name the automobile
after its locomotion, an essential aspect of its being. But the
Wintu, in his preoccupation with form alone, finds no incongruity
in classifying the automobile with the turtle as: it looks like an
inverted pot in motion. Especially illustrative of this attitude are
the words tliDiq' and -lila, which the Wintu uses in situations
where we would have used *make, create, manufacture*, or, more
colloquially, *fix*. But these English equivalents are far from the
meaning of the Wintu words; -lila, which I have often translated
as *manufacture*, actually means *to turn into, to transform;* that
is, to change one form into another. And tliDiq' does not mean
make; it means *to work on*. Our *make* often implies creation,
the tliDiq' finds matter, assumes its presence. *Make* presupposes
an act of aggression, the imposition of self upon matter; tliDiq'
also involves an act of will but one that is restrained and spends
itself on the surface.

This respect for the inviolability of the given finds further
expression in the conception of the relationship between self and
other. Two Wintu suffixes, which in English are rendered as
coercive, reflect this attitude. One of these is -i·ï or -wil, which
is used to transitivize a verb, when the object is particular.
For example, DiBa. means *to cross* (a river or ridge); DeBuwil
means *to take across* (a child, beads, weapons, etc.). But the
-i·l may also mean *to do with;* so that DeBuwil may mean *to go
across with*. There is the term be·wil, which means to *possess
something particular;* but it also means *to be with*. The initiative
is with the subject in both cases; but there is no act of aggression; there is a coordinate relationship. The word suki·l, ap-

plied to a chief, I have translated as *to rule;* but the word means
to stand with. We would say, at best, that the suffix has the two
meanings at the same time; but the Wintu makes no distinction
between the two concepts, except when he has to use a language
that reflects a habit of thought that regards this distinction as
natural.

Another suffix that, like the -i·l, deals with the relationship of
self and other is -ma·. This sometimes appears as a causative;
for example, ba· means *to eat* and ba·ma· means *to feed,* that
is, *to give to eat, to make eat.* Bira· means *to swallow;* Beruma·,
to fish with bait. But like the -i·l this too implies a coordinate
relationship, and one of great intimacy between self and other;
for example, a chief tells his people (*with the coming* of the
Whites) *you shall hunger,* bira·lebo·sken; *your children shall
hunger,* birama·lebo·sken (literally, *children you shall hunger
in respect of*). The relatives of a pubescent girl—balas—are referred to as balm·s (*they were pubescent in respect of*). A man
says, koyuma· da ila·m; kuya: is *to be ill;* the man says in effect
I am ill in respect to my child. I use *in respect to* for an other
which is not entirely separated from the self and with which
the self is intimately concerned. What we express as an act of
force is here expressed in terms of continuity between self and
other.

I have avoided advisedly the use of the term *identification*
here. This term implies an original delimitation and separation.
It is the nearest that our social scientists, starting from delimitation, can come to unity. But if the Wintu starts with an original
oneness, we must speak not of identification but of a premise
of continuity. We find this premise underlying not only linguistic categories but his thought and behavior throughout. It
is basic to the Wintu attitude toward society, for example. It
explains why kinship terms are classified, not with the sub-
stantives, but with the pronouns such as *this;* why the special
possessives used with them, such as the neD, in neDDa·n·, *my
father,* are really pronouns of participation, to be used also with
aspects of one's identity as, for example, my act, my intention,
my future death. To us, in the words of Ralph Linton, "Society

has as its foundation an aggregate of individuals." For the Wintu, the individual is a delimited part of society; it is society that is basic, not a plurality of individuals. Again, this premise of the primacy of the unpartitioned whole gives a valid basis to beliefs such as that a man will lose his hunting luck if he goes on a hunt while his wife is menstruating. Where formal distinctions are derivative and transitory, a man is at one with his wife in a way that is difficult, if not impossible, for us to appreciate.

There is further the Wintu premise of a reality beyond his delimiting experience. His experience is that of a reality as shaped by his perception and conceptualization. Beyond it is the timeless design to which his experiences have given temporality. He believes in it, and he taps it through his ritual acts and his magic, seeking luck to reinforce and validate his experiential skills and knowledge, to endow his acts with effectiveness. A hunter must have both skill and luck; but skill is the more limited. An unskilled hunter who has luck can still hit a deer by rare chance, but a skilled hunter without luck can never do so. The myths contain examples of hunters who, having lost their luck, can never kill a deer again. Now, knowledge and skill are phrased agentively and experientially; but luck is phrased passively or in terms of non-actualized reality. The hunter who has lost his luck does not *say I cannot kill deer any more*, but *Deer don't want to die for me*. The natural, reached through luck, is impersonal; it cannot be known or sensed, and it is never addressed; but not so the supernatural. It can be felt or seen; it is personal. It is within experience. Such experience can be questioned, and proof of it is often offered; the doctoring shaman produces as evidence the fish he has extracted from a patient, the missile of some supernatural being. Klutchie, a shaman, offers his knowledge of a coast language as proof that, during a protracted trance of which he has no memory, he was carried by a spirit to the West Coast. But natural necessity is beyond question and demands no proof. It is only implied; there is no name for it. The supernatural is named and can be spoken of. Toward the supernatural the Wintu performs acts of will.

The shaman, speaking to the spirit he controls, will command and demand. But the man who dives deep into a sacred pool to seek luck will say *May it happen that I win at gambling.* His request is non-agentive and impersonal; he does not address nature, neither does he command.

Recurring through all this is the attitude of humility and respect toward reality, toward nature and society. I cannot find an adequate English term to apply to a habit of thought that is so alien to our culture. We are aggressive toward reality. We say, This is bread; we do not say, as the Wintu, *I call this bread* or *I feel* or *taste* or *see it to be bread.* The Wintu never says starkly *this is;* if he speaks of reality that is not within his own restricting experience, he does not affirm it, he only implies it. If he speaks of his experience, he does not express it as categorically true. Our attitude toward nature is colored by a desire to control and exploit. The Wintu relationship with nature is one of intimacy and mutual courtesy. He kills a deer only when he needs it for his livelihood and utilizes every part of it, hoofs and marrow and hide and sinew and flesh; waste is abhorrent to him, not because he believes in the intrinsic virtue of thrift, but because the deer had died for him. A man too old to fend for himself prays:

. . . I cannot go up to the mountains in the west to you, deer;
I cannot kill you and bring you home . . .
You, water, I can never dip you up and fetch you home
again . . .
You who are wood, you wood, I cannot carry you home on
my shoulder.[1]

This is not the speech of one who has plucked the fruits of nature by brute force. In conclusion, I quote an old woman, who, speaking in sorrow of the coming of the Whites, expresses the two attitudes toward nature:

The white people never cared for land or deer or bear. When we Indians kill meat, we eat it all up. When we dig roots, we make little holes. . . . We don't chop down

[1] Dorothy Lee, "Some Indian Texts Dealing with the Supernatural," *The Review of Religion,* May, 1944, p. 407.

the trees. We only use dead wood. But the white people plow up the ground, pull up the trees, kill everything. . . . The spirt of the land hates them. They blast out trees and stir it up to its depths. They saw up the trees. That hurts them. The Indians never hurt anything. . . .[2]

[2] Cora DuBois, *Wintu Ethnography*, University of California Publications in American Archaeology and Anthropology, 36, 1935.

The following papers by the present author give the detailed material on which this paper is based. "Conceptual Implications of a Primitive Language," *Philosophy of Science*, 5:89-102, 1938; "Some Indian Texts dealing with the Supernatural," *The Review of Religion*, pp. 403-411, 1941; "Categories of the Generic and the Particular in Wintu," *American Anthropologist*, 46:362-9. For the classification of kinship terms, see: "Kinship Terms in Wintu Speech," *American Anthropologist*, 42:604-6. For words dealing with the formal rather than the kinesthetic aspect of activity, see: "The Linguistic Aspect of Wintu Acculturation," *American Anthropolgist*, 45:347-40. For material on the relationship between self and other, see: "Notes on the Conception of the Self Among the Wintu Indians," *The Journal of Abnormal and Social Psychology*, 45:3, 1950, reprinted in revised form in *Explorations 3*.

TIME AND TENSE IN SPANISH EPIC POETRY

Stephen Gilman

The *Poema del Cid*—I may remind readers whose encyclo-
pedias are out of reach—is a Spanish epic of 3,730 lines written
in the year 1140 or thereabouts. With a historical veracity un-
paralleled in the heroic poetry of the Middle Ages, it tells of
the exile from Castille of Rodrigo Díaz de Vivar, first called the
Cid (Sidi) by his Moorish antagonists. As a result of calumny
and court jealousy, the King of Castille and León, Alfonso VI,
"takes away his love" from the hero and so condemns him to
a kind of social banishment. Even worse, he orders him and
his small band of relatives and followers to leave the kingdom
within a given time. They go to the one place where such
ancestors of the "conquistadores" could go, over the border to
live by their courage and wits among the Moors. The first of the
three "cantares" gives a moving account of the Cid's initial poverty, of his first skirmishes and scuffles, and of his almost picaresque self-defense against two hostile societies. The last two
"cantares" record his increasing prosperity, his return to favor,
and his capture of Valencia as a fief—an event that was the
marvel of the age.

The end of the *Poema* is deeply in accord with Max Scheler's
doctrine that the hero by definition "enriches" the world in
value. The anonymous "juglar" in a series of moving episodes
shows how the meaning of Spain—not just Castille but, for the
first time, all Spain—has been enhanced by the Cid's version of
heroism. He is not irrational and passionately savage as are the
inhabitants of the *Nibelungenlied* nor yet an individualist of
incredible prowess and incredible rashness such as Roland.
Rather, he is practical, a family man, a natural leader with a
humorous human touch unique in the medieval world. He is a

man of sure moderate judgment and natural dignity, qualities that remind us more of the frontiersman (as given in our national typology) than of the knight. When all of this has been fully displayed in action and dialogue, one of the last verses makes explicit the meaning his person—not just his conquests and deeds —has for his people: "a todos alcança ondra por el que en buena nació." [1]

It is the Cid of the *Poema* who sets for Spain the human pattern of national values, who first represents the positing of honor on the "integral" self-maintenance of the individual in all adverse circumstances. In this the jovial and heroically successful Cid is one with the sad, ever defeated knight of the Mancha. The Cid has fulfilled his epic function for his people.

The form of the *Poema,* written for chanted recital on three successive evenings, is exceedingly irregular. Its verses are of uneven length and rhyme assonantally in equally uneven stanzas. "Laisses" is the technical term. The grammar, too, is fluid in its tracing of heroic movement. Connectives are missing; short clauses and sentences succeed each other without regard for transition; and the morphological forms vary from verse to verse. But most irregular of all—so irregular as to be almost chaotic— are the tenses of the verbs. The two regular Spanish past tenses, the preterite and the imperfect, frequently disregard the distinction of time of action driven with so much difficulty into the minds and habits of foreign students. That is to say, the "juglar" seldom makes it clear that one shows past condition and the other past conclusion. He is quite capable of replacing "Once upon a time there was [imperfect] a king who built [preterite] a tower . . ." with its reverse. Even more confusing is the frequent intermixture of presents and present perfects into the narrative stream. The following passage (translated literally and so incorrectly) will serve as an example:

They *loosed* [preterite] the reins; they *think* to go.
Near *approaches* the deadline for leaving the kingdom.
My Cid *came* [preterite] to rest in Spinaz de Can.

[1] Honor comes to all because of him who was born in a good hour." This is one of the favorite epic epithets for the Cid and serves, as we shall see, as a kind of enhanced proper name.

Many warriors *come* into his service that night from
around about.

The next day he *thinks* to ride.

The loyal Cid *is going* out of his country,
on the left Sant Estevan, a goodly city;

he *passed* [preterite] through Alcobiella which *is* already
the end of Castille;

the highroad of Quinea, he *was going* [imperfect] to
cross.

Traditionally this crazy quilt of tenses has been understood as
a sign of the "popularity" of the Cid's epic—a sign of its use
of a "popular" language to tell its story. Although the "Volks-
geist" was long ago consigned to the history of ideas, the basic
classification of poetry—particularly epic poetry—into "popular"
and "cultivated" brackets is still with us. And one of the accepted signs of such "popularity" is the indiscriminate and un-
calculated use of the "historical present" to make the narrative
more "vivid." [2] The "popular" mind—and this may be taken to
mean the mind of a poet writing for and in terms of a
"popular" audience—is as unmindful of the rules for sequence
of tenses as a Grandma Moses is of the rules of perspective.
There is no narrative point of view (to use a notion often applied to the art of that most "cultivated" of narrators, Henry
James) from which tenses can relate themselves logically to
each other. As a result, the "popular" poet uses tense according to the impulse of the moment—or, at best, according to his
instinctive appreciation of the dramatic needs of the moment.
An untutored genius, he writes a language of vital expression, a
poetry that is free from grammatical awareness of time and
space. In the words of Jacob Grimm, such a poet offers us the
fabulous gift of "life itself in pure action."

There can be no question but that this is an attractive theory.

[2] There is a kind of unquestioned rapprochement of the "historical
present" as used in popular speech to the mixture of tenses not only of the
Poema del Cid but also to that of the *Chanson de Roland*, its fellow
"chansons de gestes," as well as an infinite number of Spanish "romances"
or ballads. The fact of irrational mixture distinguishes this kind of "historical present" from the more systematic, and so more "cultivated," use
of the present by a Virgil. Actually, as I shall try to show, Virgil seems to
me much closer to a "popular" use of the present than these medieval poems.

It has all the charm of the Romanticism it reflects, all the appeal of a myth of lost freedom. Even more, as I shall try to show, it is not entirely mistaken! It is incomplete; it has been wrongly emphasized in certain respects; yet it corresponds to a certain underlying truth. Let us see first the mistaken emphasis. Bergson insists that the sequence from preliminary chaos to natural order, a habitual mental sequence derived from the myth of creation, is the cause of a great deal of erroneous thinking. There is always order, even though it may be unrecognizable from the point of view of the observer. A child's room cluttered with toys will serve as an example. The strewing of blocks and lead soldiers reflects not random disarray but the vital course of the child's existence in the room. This, I think, is the error of the neo-Romantic interpretation of the "popular" historical present. Like wistful adults, such critics view the *Poema* and poems resembling it from the point of view of an age trapped in time, space, and grammar and conscious of the trap. Hence, they stress the lost freedom to be disorderly—even acutely anarchical—and ignore the possibility of another kind of order quite alien to conventional narrative practice. "Freedom from" has been emphasized more than "freedom to. . . ."

A chance observation first indicated to me that such a hidden system or order might be found in the *Poema del Cid*.[3] I happened to notice that the sequence of tenses was regular and unexceptional (from the point of view of standard grammar) *in the dialogue*. And that means in about 45 per cent of the lines, according to the tabulation of a German scholar. Here, I thought, was a striking demonstration that the mixture of present and past was not a matter of linguistic naiveté. Instead the poet seemed to have two distinct ways of using tense: when the hero speaks he does so from his heroic point of view, and the tenses take their normal course. But when he himself narrates, he seems to discard his point of view (in this the Romantic interpretation

---

[3] For the *Chanson de Roland* (and presumably for other "chansons de geste") Anna Granville Hatcher has published sensitive and brilliant stylistic analyses of tense usage. Her interpretation, however, is based on a narrative quite different from the Spanish and so cannot be adapted for my purposes. See "Tense Usage in the *Roland*," *Studies in Philology*, 1942, and "Epic Patterns in Old French," *Word*, 1946.

is correct) in favor of some other principle of tense arrangement.
The poet, as we shall see, reverently refrains from "possessing"
the hero and his deeds from the temporal perspective of the
present. He refrains from chaining them to an irrevocable past
by adherence to the grammatical logic of his narrative position.[4]

At this point the question could be posed directly: What
was the order of tenses in the narrative? If not vital hazard,
what did each tense actually signify? The answer involved a
survey of the narrative language, into the details of which I need
not here enter. My effort was to try to discover the linguistic
circumstances most frequently accompanying the several tenses
in their ordinary usage. After months of painful tabulation, I
arrived at one suggestive relationship: when the hero was the
named subject of the sentence (a very frequent situation in this
as in all epics), the preterite tense was used four times as much
as the present.[5] Conversely, when the subject has no proper
name (this included things, groups of people, and very very in-
frequently, personal pronouns in the singular), the present replaced the preterite by a margin almost as wide. Thus, these
two tenses seemed to depend more on the subject of the sentence
than on the time—past or present—of action. There was here an
apparent principle of stylistic order—apart from the poet's
"popular" or "naive" freedom to circumvent time.

Readers familiar with noncivilized cultures will have already
suspected the nature of this principle. They will have recognized
in this subject-tense correlation a sign of the extraordinary—and
frequently magical—importance that the name can have. This
is specially true of heroic poetry from the *Iliad* to the ballads
of our own time. In poetry as well as magic, the name is in a

---

[4] Theorists agree (and the notion goes back as far as Hesiod, according
to Bowra) that the epic refers by its very nature to a past Epic Age, to a
past of superhuman "Homeric" virtue and prowess. Yet the very stressing
of this pastness involves a counter-stress on "presentation," on "invoking"
for present wonder and possible imitation. The past is important to the
present and becomes a myth to be relived by the present. It must not,
therefore, be thought of archaeologically or picturesquely (in the manner of
a Scott). That is to say, it must not be thought of as wholly and irretrievably
past.

[5] The same thing holds true for the secondary heroes as well as other
properly named subjects.

real sense an invocation that brings the hero and his deeds up out of the past. It is not a sign. It belongs to the heroic essence —and it is significant in this connection that the war cry of the Cid is a kind of self-invocation. The Spanish hero brings terror to the Moors and courage to his own handful of fellow exiles by proclaiming: "I am Ruy Díaz, the Cid of Bivar, the Fighter." It is a name that the poet never tires of using (with numberless variations of epithet) and that the listener never tires of hearing. It is his assurance that the epic is not a fiction but, rather, encloses profound and specific human truth. Only in his name can a hero be "celebrated" epically, for only in his name can his unique value be expressed. Praise and flattery imply comparison, elevation of the person praised on a given hierarchy of values, whereas heroism is essentially incomparable. The hero creates values in his action—values so unique that to praise them is impossible. They can only be "celebrated" in the naming of the doer and his deeds. In this sense, one might call "A rose is a rose is a rose" a "celebrative" lyric.[6]

But why the preterite tense? Castro remarks in the *Structure of Spanish History*[7] that the grammar of the *Poema* is axiological rather than logical. As a narrative, its parts are arranged in terms of value estimations (like a medieval painting in which the most important saint is the biggest) and not in terms of sequence and consequence. In other words, the preterite is the tense of action by the named hero because it expresses in some way the special value of his action. It is a tense that communicates importance instead of time—a tense that is not really a "tense" at all, just as the gold of a painted halo is not really a color. The present, on the other hand, used with those sentence subjects which are not "celebrated" in their names is of lesser value. Rather than narrating

---

[6] One of the most striking results of this heroic uniqueness is the fact that heroes are so frequently bad from the point of view of ethics (that is to say, systematized values). Although the Cid is far removed from a Hagen or a Raoul de Cambrai in this sense, he can stoop to a picaresque confidence trick without the slightest self-questioning.

[7] This book, replete with seed intuitions for the human sciences, has just been published in translation by the Princeton University Press. Its profound integration of history with culture, deserves the attention of anthropologists and sociologists as well as historians.

more vividly (as the "historical present" is supposed to do), it is a filler tense, a background tense from which the preterites stand out in stylistic relief.

These statements are mere assumptions—as vague as the Romantic generalizations they replace—until they are realized in our experience with the text. Since here such an experience must be prefabricated, the following will have to do. The Cid is sleeping in his palace in Valencia; a lion has escaped from the palace zoo:

> The followers of the Cid *furl* their capes on their arms,
> And they *surround* the couch of their lord; they *stay* there
>   [to protect him] . . .
> At this moment He who was born in a good hour *awoke,*
> *saw* his couch surrounded by his good vassals:
> "What is this men? What do you want?"
> "Oh, honored sir, the lion frightened us."
> My Cid *leaned* on his elbow; rose to his feet;
> *has* his own cape hanging at his neck; and *headed*
>   straight for the lion.

The feeling for tableau, for pictorial hierarchy, is evident even in this fragment of episode; but we must also notice that its movement—in accord with the demands of the genre—is continuous. On the one hand, there is the movement of the nameless vassals described by the narrator in the present tense. On the other, there is the preterite action sequence of the hero who "awoke," who "saw," who "raised himself on one elbow" (to see the lion), who "rose to his feet," and "who headed straight for the lion." There is something special, something self-determined in this decisive preterite action—action of which each gesture and successive phase is underlined for our admiration. If the vassals are described in the present, the Cid is celebrated in the preterite. There is, of course, one apparent exception—the cape that the Cid "has hanging" at his neck in the present (since he disdains to protect himself with it as do his vassals). Yet this is precisely something that the Cid doesn't do, action that he refuses to accomplish and, hence, is hardly to be celebrated. Both the narrative movement—with its almost pictorial contrast of vassal to lord—and the narrative grammar—with its contrast of present and preterite tenses—are clearly axiological.

Confronted with this rejection of the "historical present," the surprised grammarian will hardly admit that "axiology" is an acceptable substitute. If the temporal interpretation of tense is to be discarded, he will ask, what replaces it? Or more simply, why and how is the preterite used as if it were more valuable than the present? My answer is one that is suggested by contemporary trends of grammatical thinking: the tenses of the *Poema* are used aspectually, as if they were not tenses at all but aspects. The preterite is, of course, traditionally perfective. It expresses concluded, accomplished, "perfect" action—that is to say, the kind of action that constitutes the heroic "deed." The hero doesn't doubt, feel moody, or exist inconclusively. The antithesis of a hypochondriac, psychic delay is alien to his being. His value resides in doing, in completing acts one after another, and there can be no question but that the perfectivity of the preterite becomes him. As for the present, its failure to indicate completion one way or another suits better those nameless subjects whose role is not to start and finish action on their own but to obey. It is the tense of those subjects who are described —like the worried vassals of the lion episode—as they arrange themselves about the heroic prime mover.[8]

This notion of evaluative or stylistic aspects is confirmed neatly by the verbs that are used with the Cid as subject. A French linguist remarks that "there are certain verbs for which a story teller will abandon past time and go into the present: *il entre, il sort, il part, il s'arrête.* . . ."[9] The historical present is for orthodox grammatical thinking a means to vivid energetic action and only disappears when the "life" of the story is "sus-

[8] As I have already mentioned, this category of "nameless" subjects includes not only the groups, the vassals and soldiers under the Cid's command, but also singular and even inanimate subjects. All together these things make up the narrative world, a world that, unlike that of the novel, is never described for its own sake. Within the epic narrative its only purpose is to be acted upon and to provide a place for heroism. It is just the opposite of an "environment" and so refrains from creating experience or influencing action.

[9] Buffin, *La durée et le temps en français,* Paris, 1925. Buffin elaborates upon but does not contradict the accepted notion of the historical present as presented, for example, by Brugmann.

pended in favor of description." The point is that the verbs that
specialize in the historical present are not at all the same as those
put into the present in the *Poema*. The French verbs listed are
all perfective, verbs that conclude themselves as they are used,
while in the *Poema* the verbs preferring the present (three to
one over the preterite) are imperfective: "to think," "to go," "to
be able," "to have." They are verbs that denote a process or
condition instead of an act begun and finished. Conversely, it
is the "active, vivid, energetic, lively" verbs that are used with
the Cid and put into the preterite (70 and 80 per cent of the
time). The situation is, in fact, just the reverse of that which
the notion of historical present might lead us to expect. The
most familiar use of the English "popular" historical present is
with the verb "to say": "he says . . . and then she says. . . ."
But in the *Poema* "decir" is used 92 times in the preterite and
only 17 times in the present.[10]

Thus, the Cid has not only his own tense but also his own
kind of verbs. He is an active agent not only in the story but
also in the way the story is told. With his high frequency of
preterites and with his overwhelming choice of perfective verbs,
he penetrates the very process of narration. In the invocation
of his name—"mío Cid Ruy Díaz de Bivar, el que en buen ora
çinxo espada"—he dominates one sentence after another and
almost seems to push the narrator aside. This is, of course, not
a new thing to say about epic poetry. In one of the most famous
passages of the *Laocöon*, Lessing remarks on the "active" poetry
of the *Iliad*. Homer, he says, does not himself describe how
Agamemnon is dressed; rather, he lets the hero put on his clothes
item by item as the active named subject of the narrative.[11]
Heroes are beyond description; they can only be celebrated in
their autonomous self-generated action, in their "activation" of

[10] The use of "decir" in the present is frequent in other non-epic genres
of Old Spanish poetry—such as the famous *Libro de buen amor*. But in the
Poema the value of saying cannot be communicated by the present. "Then
he says . . ." implies an attitude quite antithetical to "Achilles spoke
winged words. . . ."
[11] There is an identical treatment of the Cid's dress in the *Poema*. It is
a coincidence beyond the range of conceivable influence which may be
attributed to the generic similarity of the two narratives. Gestures and dress
as well as battles are the recurrent foci of epic celebration.

the poetic narrative. As for their poets, they have traditionally relegated themselves to anonymity. In the words of the Spanish novelist, Valle Inclán, they "write on their knees."

Such, I maintain, is the hidden order of the tenses in the *Poema del Cid*. When the Cid is subject he is celebrated with perfective verbs and in a perfective tense; he is celebrated insofar as he initiates and completes deeds in his own name. But when the persons and artifacts of the narrative world take command of the sentences, the verbs are imperfective and the tense present. The poet no longer need stand aside in an attitude of celebrative reverence. He can describe "background" (perhaps "foundation" or "circumstance" would be better words) with direct and dramatic effectiveness. The two major tenses of the *Poema* are thus two aspects, perfective and imperfective.[12] They are also stylistic indicators of narrative importance, and as such they correspond to alternate attitudes of admiration and intervention—celebration and description—on the part of the poet. He enters in the present and withdraws in the preterite, thereby converting the two tenses into "stylistic aspects." That is to say, aspects that, like all classic components of style, reflect the prevailing value level or "decorum" of the poem.[13]

The *Poema del Cid* is unquestionably an epic and reflects in its style the recurrent conditions of epic creation. It is also unique, as unique in its use of tense as in its moderate historical hero. And I may conclude this discussion with some uneducated

[12] The third major tense, the imperfect, is also used aspectually, a situation that will hardly surprise contemporary theorists who have in several different ways sought to divorce this tense from time. Its function in the *Poema* is quite distinct from the present, however—as I try to show in the monograph on which this article is based.

[13] In the narrative style of the *Poema*, it is, of course, impossible to "fix" a given tense, to establish a single connotation that will hold for its every occurrence. Many preterites are used in a manner that would be hard to distinguish from that of an ordinary narrative—the temporal use of tense being a recurrent possibility for the poet. In other individual cases, the preterite seems only to indicate perfectivity and to each special evaluative commitment. Finally, there are a great many instances (such as those translated from the lion episode) in which the indication of conclusion is less important than the indication of value or importance. These are the most interesting stylistically and may be understood as a kind of "intensive." For the determination of these qualities, ordinary linguistic and statistical analysis is insufficient. The curious feature of such a study as this is that it begins with statistics and ends with intuition—and on that account will probably satisfy nobody.

guessing as to why and how. The only text I know in Spanish that uses tense in a fashion at all similar to the *Poema* is a 16th century translation of the *Song of Songs*. In his commentary the translator, the exquisite humanist, poet, and mystic, Fray Luis de León, indicates that he uses the preterite to render the Hebrew intensive aspect—in spite of all temporal anomaly. And if this is consciously done in the 16th century, is it not possible that a Castille that had already "coexisted" with Semitic culture for four centuries should more or less unconsciously assimilate Semitic aspects to its narrative techniques? Castro's brilliant discussion of the interpenetration of Moorish and Christian cultures gives the strongest kind of support to such an assumption.[14] And Edmund Wilson's remarks on the intensives of the Old Testament by this time sound familiar:

> When Enoch or Noah "walks with God," he does so in this form of the verb "to walk" and nobody has ever known how to render it. Yet one gets from the Hebrew original the impression that the walking of these patriarchs was of a very special kind, that it had the effect of making them more important and more highly charged.[15]

My guess—uneducated because I know no aspectual language at first hand—is precisely this: that aspect, in the Semitic Orient a means of value communication, has been assimilated in typical Spanish fashion to the primary Occidental genre, the epic.[16]

[14] Among the many lines of investigation traced in *The Structure of Spanish History* is the impingement of Arabic on Spanish, an impingement that Castro demonstrates as going much deeper than lexicographical borrowing. Following Castro's lead, T. B. Irving, in "Completion and Becoming in the Spanish Verb," *Modern Languages Journal*, 1953, goes so far as to propose a full syntactical invasion of Arabic aspects into a number of Spanish constructions.

[15] *New Yorker*, May 15, 1954.

[16] I suspect that scholars who find epics in all sorts of noncivilized cultures use the term so loosely as to render it useless for literary criticism. The human and mortal heroism of the Occidental epic (from the *Iliad* to the great medieval poems) is a central exigency of the genre affecting form and theme. As Lascelles Abercrombie shows (*The Epic*, London, 1914), without this basic definition of heroism, any kind of mythological or adventuresome poem (or motion picture) can be thought of as epic. As for the lack of epic in the Arabic world, Castro remarks: "Furthermore, in Arabic literature the characters are dissolved in the narrated event, they are transformed into metaphorical expression or into moral wisdom; they never stand out "sculpturally" against other characters or against their environment. Neither characters nor things have sharply chiseled existences.

The epic was, indeed, the one kind of narrative to which aspects could be assimilated, for as the Romantics knew, it lacked a point of view, a single perspective from which tenses could be anchored in sequence. Its technique of celebration resulted in freedom—freedom to introduce a new grammatical order, a way of expressing value that was alien to the time of the West.

To feel the presence of a character presupposes feeling him as present and not as flowing through timeless time or unwinding in a continuous arabesque from one happening to another. . . . Islam has no notion of existence in terms of a life that believes itself to be autonomous" (*The Structure of Spanish History*, p. 287). Hence, the lack of "heroism" in the epic sense of the term. When Averroes, the great Arabic commentator and transmitter of Aristotle to the Western World, came to the *Poetics* his interpretation of the theory of tragedy and the tragic hero was highly inaccurate but still recognizable. For the epic, however, he broke down altogether: "Aristotle describes the difference between the tragedy and the epic and explains which poets were best in each or which were unfortunate and unskillful and praises Homer above all the others. But this is a matter proper to the Greeks and among us there is not to be found anything of the sort either because [the epic] is not common to all people or because something supernatural has influenced the Arabs in this connection. The gentiles have in their "imitations" their own customs according to period and region." I translate from the Spanish of Menéndez Pelayo who in turn translates from the Latin translation (*Historia de la ideas estéticas en España II*, Madrid, 1928, p. 154).

BUDDHIST SYMBOLISM

Daisetz T. Suzuki

Basho, one of the greatest *haiku* poets in 18th century Japan, produced this when his eyes for the first time opened to the poetic and philosophical significance of *haiku*:

> *Furuike-ya!*
> *Kawazu tobi-komu*
> *Mizu-no oto!*
>
> Oh! Old pond!
> A frog leaps in,
> The water's sound!

This is, as far as its literary sense goes, no more than a simple statement of the fact. Here is the ancient pond, probably partly covered with some aquatic plants and bordered with the bushes and weeds rampantly growing. The clear spring water, serenely undisturbed, reflects the trees with their fresh green foliage of the springtime, enhanced by a recent rainfall. A little green frog comes out of the grass and jumps into the water, giving rise to a series of ripples growing larger and larger until they touch the banks. The little frog jumping into the water should not make much of a sound. But when it takes place in a quiet environment it cannot pass unnoticed by Basho, who was in all likelihood absorbed in deep contemplation of nature. However feeble the sound might have been, it was enough to awaken him from his meditation. So he set down in the seventeen-syllable *haiku* what went through his consciousness.

Now the question is: What was this experience Basho, the poet, had at the moment?

As far as the *haiku* itself is concerned, it does not go beyond the matter-of-fact statement of the phenomenon of which he was the witness. There is no reference to what may be termed the subjective aspect of the incident except the little particle, *ya*. Indeed, the presence of *ya* is the key word to the whole composition. With this the *haiku* ceases to be an objective description of the frog jumping into the old pond and of the sound of the water caused thereby.

So long as the old pond remains a container of a certain volume of water quietly reflecting the things around it, there is no life in it. To assert itself as reality, a sound must come out of it; a frog jumps into it, the old pond then proves to be dynamic, to be full of vitality, to be of significance to us sentient beings. It becomes an object of interest, of value.

But there is one important observation we have to make, which is that the value of the old pond to Basho, the poet and seer (or mystic), did not come from any particular source outside the pond but from the pond itself. It may be better to say, the pond is the value. The pond did not become significant to Basho because of his finding the value in the pond's relationship to anything outside the pond as a pond.

To state this in other words, the frog's jumping into the pond, its causing the water to splash and make a noise, was the occasion—intellectually, dualistically, or objectively speaking—to make Basho realize that he was the pond and the pond was he, and that whatever value there was in this identification, the value was no other than the fact of this identification itself. There was nothing added to the fact.

When he recognized the fact, the fact itself became significant. Nothing was added to it. The pond was a pond, the frog was a frog, the water was water. The objects remained the same. No, it is better to express the idea in this way: no objective world, so called, at all existed with its frogs, ponds, etc., until one day a person known as Basho came suddenly to the scene and heard "the water's sound." The scene, indeed, until then had no existence. When its value was recognized by Basho this was to Basho the beginning or the creation of an objective world. Before this, the old pond was there as if it were not in existence. It was no more than a dream; it had no reality. It was the occasion of Basho's hearing the frog that the whole world, including the poet himself, sprung out of Nothingness *ex nihilo*.

There is still another way of describing Basho's experience and the birth of an objective world.

In their moment there was no participation, on the part of Basho, in the life of the old pond or of the little green frog. Both subject and object were totally annihilated. And yet the pond was the pond, Basho was Basho, the frog was the frog; they remained as they were, or as they have been from the beginningless past. And yet Basho was no other than the pond when he faced the pond; Basho was no other than the frog when he heard the sound of the water caused by its leaping. The leaping, the sound, the frog, and the pond, and Basho were all in one and one in all. There was an absolute totality, that is, an absolute identity, or, to use Buddhist terminology, a perfect state of emptiness (i.e., *Sunyata*) or suchness (i.e., *Tathata*). Intellectualists or logicians may declare that all these different objects of nature are symbols, as far as Basho is concerned, of the highest value of reality. That this is not the view I have tried to explain is quite evident, I believe.

Why did Basho exclaim, *"Furuike-ya!"* "Oh! Old pond!"? What significance does this *"ya!"*, corresponding to the English "Oh!" in this case, have to the rest of the *haiku*? The particle has the force of singling out the old pond from the rest of the objects or events and of making it the special point of reference. Thus, when the pond is mentioned, not only the series of events as particularly mentioned in the *haiku* but also an infinite inexhaustible totality of things making up the human world of existence comes along with it. The old pond of Basho is the Dharmadhatu in the Kegon system of Buddhist philosophy. The whole pond contains the whole cosmos, and the whole cosmos finds itself securely held in the pond.

This idea may be illustrated by an infinite series of natural numbers. When we pick up any one of these numbers, for example, 5, we know that it is 1 (one) so many times repeated, that this repetition is not merely mechanical but originally related, and, therefore, that the series is an organic whole so closely and solidly united that when any one of the numbers is missing the whole series ceases to be a series (or group), and, further, that each unit thus represents or symbolizes the whole.

Take a number designated 5. 5 is not just 5. It is organically related to the rest of the series. 5 is 5 because of its being related to all the other numbers as units and also to the series as a whole. Without this 5 the whole is no more a whole, nor can all the other units (6, 4, 7, 8, 9, etc.) be considered belonging to the series. 5, then, not only contains in it all the rest of the numbers in the infinite series; it is also the series itself. It is in this sense when the Buddhist philosophy states that all is one and one is all, or that the one is the many and the many the one.

Basho's *haiku* of "the old pond" now becomes perhaps more intelligible. The old pond with the frog jumping into it and producing a sound, which not only spatially but temporally reaches the end of the world, is in the *haiku* by no means the ordinary pond we find everywhere in Japan, and the frog, too, is no common "green frog" of the springtime. To the author of the *haiku* "I" am the old pond, "I" am the frog, "I" am the sound, "I" am reality itself, including all these separate individual units of existence. Basho at this moment of spiritual exaltation is the universe itself; nay, he is God Himself, Who uttered the fiat, "Let there be light." The fiat corresponds to "the sound of the water," for it is from this "sound" that the whole world takes its rise.

This being so, do we call "the old pond" or the water's sound or the leaping frog a symbol for the ultimate reality? In Buddhist philosophy there is nothing behind the old pond, because it is complete in itself and does not point to anything behind or beyond or outside itself. The old pond (or the water or the frog) itself is reality.

If the old pond is to be called a symbol because of its being an object of sense, intellectually speaking, then the frog is a symbol, the sound is a symbol, the pen with which I write this is a symbol, the paper is a symbol, the writer is a symbol; indeed, the whole world is a symbol, including what we designate "reality." Symbolism may thus go on indefinitely.

Buddhist symbolism would therefore declare that everything is symbolic, it carries meaning with it, it has values of its own, it exists by its own right pointing to no reality other than itself. Fowls of the air and lilies of the field are the divine glory itself.

They do not exist because of God. God Himself cannot exist
without them, if God is assumed to be existing somewhere.

An old learned Chinese dignitary once said to a Zen master:
"Chuangtze announces that heaven and earth are one horse, the
ten thousand things are one finger; is this not a wonderful remark?" The master without answering this pointed at a flower
in the courtyard and said: "People of the world see the flower
as if in a dream."

Zen Buddhism avoids generalization and abstraction. When
we say that the whole world is one finger or that at the end
of a hair Mount Sumeru dances, this is an abstraction. It is
better to say with the ancient Zen master that we fail to see
the flower as it is, for our seeing is as if in a dream. We see
the flower as a symbol and not as reality itself. To Buddhists,
being is meaning. Being and meaning are one and not separable;
the separation or bifurcation comes from intellection, and intellection distorts the suchness of things.

There is another *haiku* giving the Buddhist idea of symbolization. This was composed by a woman poet of the 19th
century. It runs like this:

> *Asagao-ya!*
> *Tsurube torarete*
> *Morai mizu.*

> Oh! The morning glory!
> The bucket seized away,
> I beg for water.

When the poet early in the morning went out to draw water
from a well situated outdoors, she found the bucket entwined
by a morning glory in bloom. She was so deeply impressed by
the beauty of the flower that she forgot all about her mission.
She just stood before it. When she recovered from the shock or
trance, as it were, the only words she could utter were: "Oh!
The morning glory!" She did not describe the flower. She merely
exclaimed as she did. No reference whatever to its beauty, to its
ethereal beauty, did she make, showing how deeply, how
thoroughly, she was impressed by it. She was, in fact, carried
away by it; she was the flower and the flower was she. They

were so completely one that she lost her identity. It was only
when she woke from the moment of unconscious identity that
she realized that she was the flower itself or rather Beauty
itself. If she were a poet standing before it and admiring its
beauty, she would never have exclaimed "Oh! The morning
glory!" But as soon as she regained consciousness all that comes
out of it inevitably followed, and she suddenly remembered that
she was by the well because she wanted some water for her
morning work. Hence the remaining two lines:

> The bucket seized away,
> I beg for water.

It may be noted that the poet did not try to undo the entwining
vine. If she had wanted to, this could have been easily done, for
the morning glory yields readily to this process without being
hurt. But evidently she had no desire to touch the flower with
her earthly hands. She lovingly left it as it was. She went to her
neighbor to get the necessary water. She says the bucket was
seized away by the flower. It is remarkable that she does not
make any reference whatever to her defiling the transcendental
beauty of the thing she sees before her. It was her womanly
tenderness and passivity to refer to the captivity of the bucket.

Here again we see that there is no symbolism, for to the
poet the morning glory does not symbolize beauty; it is beauty
itself; it does not point to what is beautiful or of value; it is value
itself. There is no value to be sought outside the morning glory.
Beauty is not something to be conceived beyond the flower. It
is not a mere idea that is to be symbolized or concretized in
the morning glory. The morning glory is the whole thing. It is
not that the poet comes to beauty through or by means of what
our senses and intellect distinguish as individual objects. The
poet knows no other beauty than the morning glory as she stands
beside it. The flower is beauty itself: the poet is beauty itself.
Beauty recognizes beauty, beauty finds itself in beauty. It is
because of human senses and intellect that we have to bifurcate
beauty and talk about one who sees a beautiful object. As long
as we cling to this way of thinking, there is symbolism. But
Buddhist philosophy demands not to be blindfolded by so-called

sense objects, for they will forever keep us away from reality itself.

We see, therefore, that there is something corresponding in Buddhism to what is ordinarily known as symbolism. Buddhism is, so to speak, thoroughly realistic in the sense that it does not symbolize any particular object in distinction to something else. Buddhists would assert that if there is anything at all to be distinguished as a symbol bearing a specific value, the value here referred to has no realistic sense whatever. For there can be no such object to be specifically distinguishable. If anything is a symbol, everything is also equally a symbol, thus putting a stop to symbolism. Symbolism in Buddhist philosophy may be said to be of a different connotation from what philosophers generally understand by the term.

THE LANGUAGE OF POETRY

Northrop Frye

There are two aspects to the form of any work of literary art. In the first place, it is unique, a *techne* or artifact, to be examined by itself and without immediate reference to other things like it. In the second place, it is one of a class of similar forms. *Oedipus Rex* is in one sense not like any other tragedy, but it belongs to the class called tragedy. To understand what one tragedy is, therefore, leads us insensibly into the question of what an aspect of literature as a whole is. With this idea of the external relations of a form, two considerations in criticism become important: convention and genre.

The central principle of orthodox or Aristotelian criticism is that a poem is an imitation, the basis of imitation being, according to the *Physics*, nature. This principle, though a perfectly sound one, is still a principle that isolates the individual poem. And it is clear that any poem may be examined, not only as an imitation of nature, but as an imitation of other poems. Virgil discovered, according to Pope, that following nature was ultimately the same thing as following Homer. Once we think of a poem in relation to other poems, we begin to develop a criticism based on that aspect of symbolism which relates poems to one another, choosing, as its main field of operations, conventional or recurring images.

All art is equally conventionalized, but we do not ordinarily notice this unless we are unaccustomed to the convention. In our day the conventional element in literature is elaborately disguised by a law of copyright pretending that every work of art is an invention distinctive enough to be patented. To demonstrate the debt of A to B may get C his doctorate if A is dead, but may land him in a libel suit if A is alive. This state of things

43

makes it difficult to appraise a literature that includes Chaucer, much of whose poetry is translated or paraphrased from others; Shakespeare, whose plays sometimes follow their sources almost verbatim; and Milton, who asked for nothing better than to copy as much as possible out of the Bible. It is not only the inexperienced reader who looks for a *residual* originality in such works: most of us tend to think of a poet's real achievement as distinct from, or even contrasted with, the achievement present in what he stole. But the central greatness of, for instance, *Paradise Regained* is not the greatness of the rhetorical decorations that Milton added to his source but the greatness of the theme itself, which Milton *passes on* to the reader from his source.

The new poem, like the new baby, is born into an already existing order and is typical of the structure of poetry, which is ready to receive it. The notion that convention shows a lack of feeling, and that the poet attains "sincerity" (which usually means articulate emotion) by disregarding it, is opposed to all the facts of literary experience and history. A serious study of literature soon shows that the real difference between the original and the imitative poet is that the former is more profoundly imitative. Originality returns to the origins of literature; radicalism returns to its roots. T. S. Eliot's remark that bad poets imitate and good poets steal affords a more balanced view of convention, as it indicates that the poem is specifically involved with other poems, not vaguely with such abstractions as tradition or style. The copyright law makes it difficult for a modern novelist to steal anything except his title from the rest of literature; hence it is often only in such titles as *For Whom the Bell Tolls* or *The Sound and the Fury* that we can clearly see how much impersonal dignity and richness of association an author gains by the communism of convention.

As with other products of divine activity, the father of a poem is much more difficult to identify than the mother. That the mother is always nature, the objective considered as a field of communication, no serious criticism can ever deny. But as long as the father of a poem is assumed to be the poet himself, we fail to distinguish literature from discursive verbal structures.

The discursive writer writes as an act of conscious will; and that conscious will, along with the symbolic system he employs for it, is set over against the body of things he is describing. But the poet, who writes creatively rather than deliberately, is not the father of his poem; he is at best a midwife, or, more accurately still, the womb of Mother Nature herself: her privates he, so to speak. The true father or shaping spirit of the poem is the form of the poem itself, and this form is a manifestation of the universal spirit of poetry, the "onlie begetter" of Shakespeare's sonnets who was not Shakespeare himself, much less that depressing ghost Mr. W. H., but Shakespeare's subject, the master-mistress of his passion. When a poet speaks of the *internal* spirit that shapes the poem, he is apt to drop the traditional appeal to female Muses and think of himself as in a feminine, or at least receptive, relation to some god or lord, whether Apollo, Dionysus, Eros, Christ, or (as in Milton) the Holy Spirit. "Est *deus* in nobis," Ovid says: in modern times we may compare Nietzsche's remarks about his inspiration in *Ecce Homo*.

The problem of convention is the problem of how art can be communicable. Poetry, taken as a whole, is not simply an aggregate of artifacts imitating nature but one of the activities of human artifice taken as a whole. If we may use the word "civilization" for this, we may postulate a phase of criticism that looks at poetry as one of the techniques of civilization. It is concerned, therefore, with the social aspect of poetry, with poetry as the focus of a community.

The symbol in this phase is the communicable unit, to which I give the name archetype: that is, a typical or recurring image. I mean by an archetype a symbol that connects one poem with another and so helps to unify and integrate our literary experience. By the study of conventions and genres, it attempts to fit poems into the body of poetry as a whole.

The repetition of certain common images of physical nature like the sea or the forest in a large number of poems cannot in itself be called even "coincidence," which is the name we give to a motif when we cannot find a cause for it. But it does indicate a certain unity in the nature that poetry imitates. And when pastoral images are deliberately employed in *Lycidas*, for instance, merely because they are conventional, we can see that the convention of the pastoral makes us assimilate these images to other parts of literature. *Lycidas* leads us immediately to the whole pastoral tradition from Theocritus and Virgil down through Spenser and Milton himself to Shelley, Arnold, and Whitman, and extends into the pastoral symbolism of the Bible, of Shakespeare's forest comedies, and so on endlessly. We can get a whole literary education simply by picking up one conventional poem and following its archetypes as they stretch out into the rest of literature. And if we do not accept this archetypal element in the imagery linking different poems together, it seems to me impossible to get any systematic mental training out of the study of literature alone.

The conception of copyright extends to a general unwillingness on the part of authors of the copyright age to have their imagery studied conventionally. In dealing with this period, many archetypes have to be established by critical inspection alone. To give a random example, one very common convention of the 19th century novel is the use of two heroines, one dark and one light. The dark one is as a rule passionate, haughty, plain, foreign, or Jewish, and is in some way associated with the undesirable or with some kind of forbidden fruit like incest. When the two are involved with the same hero, the plot usually has to get rid of the dark one or make her into a sister if the story is to end happily. Examples include *Ivanhoe, The Last of the Mohicans, The Woman in White, Ligeia, Pierre* (a tragedy because the hero chooses the dark girl, who is also his sister), *The Marble Faun,* and countless incidental treatments. A male version forms the symbolic basis of *Wuthering Heights.* This device is as much convention as Milton's calling Edward King by a name out of Virgil's *Eclogues,* but it shows a confused, or, as we say, "unconscious" approach to conventions.

An archetype is not a simple but a variable convention. Archetypes are associative clusters and include a large number of specific learned associations that are communicable because a large number of people within a culture happen to be familiar with them. When we speak of symbolism in ordinary life we usually think of such learned cultural archetypes as the cross or the crown, or of such conventional associations as white with purity or green with jealousy. Such archetypes differ from signs in being complex variables: as an archetype, green may symbolize hope or vegetable nature or a go sign in traffic or Irish patriotism as easily as jealousy, but the word "green" as a verbal sign always refers to a certain color. The resistance of modern writers to having their archetypes "spotted," so to speak, is partly due to a natural anxiety to keep them as versatile as possible, not pinned down exclusively to one interpretation, a practice that would allegorize their work into a set of esoteric signs.

At one extreme of literature we have the pure convention, which a poet uses merely because it has often been used before in the same way. This is most frequent in naive poetry, in the fixed epithets and phrase-tags of medieval romance and ballad, in the invariable plots and character types of naive drama. At the other extreme we have the pure variable, where there is a deliberate attempt at novelty or unfamiliarity, and consequently a disguising or complicating of archetypes. This last is closely connected with a distrust of communication itself as a function of literature, such as appears in some forms of dadaism. It is clear that archetypes are most easily studied in highly conventionalized literature; that is, for the most part, naive, primitive, and popular literature. In suggesting the possibility of archetypal criticism, then, I am suggesting the possibility of extending the kind of comparative study now made of folk tales and ballads into the rest of literature. This should be more easily conceivable now that it is no longer fashionable to mark off popular and primitive literature from ordinary literature as sharply as we used to do.

In the general Aristotelian or neo-Classical view of poetry, as expounded, for instance, by Sidney, the events of poetry are examples and its ideas precepts. (The vagaries of English make "exemplary" the adjective for both words.) In the exemplary event there is an element of *recurrence*, something that happens time and again; in the precept, or statement about what ought to be, there is a strong element of *desire*. These elements of recurrence and desire come into the foreground in archetypal criticism. From this point of view, the narrative aspect of literature is a recurrent act of symbolic communication: in other words a ritual. Narrative (Aristotle's *mythos*) is studied by the archetypal critic as ritual or imitation of significant human action as a whole, and not simply as a *mimesis praxeos* or imitation of *an* action. Similarly, in archetypal criticism the significant content (Aristotle's *dianoia* or "thought") takes the form of the conflict of desire and reality, which has for its basis the work of the dream.

The union of ritual and dream in a form of verbal communication is usually called myth. The myth accounts for, and makes communicable, the ritual and the dream. Ritual, by itself, cannot account for itself: it is pre-logical, pre-verbal, and in a sense pre-human. Myth is distinctively human, as the most intelligent partridge cannot tell even the absurdest story explaining why it drums in the mating season. Similarly, the dream, by itself, is a system of cryptic allusions to the dreamer's own life, not fully understood by him or, so far as we know, of any real use to him. But in all dreams there is a mythical element that has a power of independent communication, as is obvious not only in the stock example of Oedipus but also in any collection of folk tales.

We may see two aspects of myth: structural or narrative myths with a ritual content, and modal or emblematic myths with a dream content. The former are most easily seen in drama, not so much in the drama of the educated audience and the settled theatre as in naive or spectacular drama: in the folk play, the puppet show, the pantomime, the farce, the pageant, and their descendants in masque, comic opera, commercial movie, and revue. Modal myths are best studied in naive romance, which includes the folk tales and fairy tales that are so closely related to dreams of wonderful wishes coming true and to nightmares of ogres and witches. The close relation of romance to ritual can be seen in the number of medieval romances that are linked to some part of the calendar—the winter solstice, a May morning, or a saint's eve. The fact that the archetype is primarily a *communicable* symbol accounts for the ease with which ballads and folk tales and mimes travel through the world, like so many of their heroes, over all barriers of language and culture. We come back here to the basis of archetypal criticism in primitive and popular literature.

By "primitive" and "popular" I mean possessing the ability to communicate in time and space respectively. Otherwise they mean much the same thing. Popular art is normally decried as vulgar by the cultivated people of its time; then it loses favor with its original audience as a new generation grows up; then it begins to merge into the softer lighting of "quaint," and cultivated people become interested in it; and finally it begins to take on the archaic dignity of the primitive. This sense of the archaic recurs whenever we find great art using popular forms, as Shakespeare does in his last period, or as the Bible does when it ends in a fairy tale about a damsel in distress, a hero killing dragons, a wicked witch, and a wonderful city glittering with jewels. In fact archaism is a regular feature of all social uses of archetypes. Soviet Russia is very proud of its production of tractors, but it will be some time before the tractor replaces the sickle on the Soviet flag.

As the archetypal critic is concerned with ritual and dream, it is likely that he would find much of interest in the work done by contemporary anthropology in ritual and by contemporary psychology in dreams. Specifically, the work done on the ritual basis of naive drama in Frazer's *The Golden Bough* and the work done on the dream basis of naive romance by Jung and the Jungians are of most direct value to him. But the three subjects of anthropology, psychology, and literary criticism are not yet clearly separated. *The Golden Bough* has had perhaps even more influence in literary criticism than in anthropology, and it may yet prove to be really a work of literary criticism. From the literary point of view, *The Golden Bough* is an essay on the ritual content of naive drama: it reconstructs an archetypal ritual from which the structural and generic principles of drama may be *logically*, not chronologically, derived. To the critic, the archetypal ritual is hypothesis, not history. It is very probable that Frazer's hypothetical ritual would have many and striking analogies to actual rituals, and collecting such analogies is part of his argument. But an analogy is not necessarily a source, an influence, a cause, or an embryonic form, much less an identity. The *literary* relation of ritual to drama is a relation of content to form, not of source to derivation.

The work of the Classical scholars who have followed Frazer's lead has produced a general theory of the spectacular or ritual content of Greek drama. But if the ritual pattern is in the plays, the critic need not take sides in the quite separate historical controversy over the ritual *origin* of Greek drama. It is, on the other hand, a matter of simple observation that the action of *Iphigeneia in Tauris,* for example, is concerned with human sacrifice. Ritual, as the content of action, and more particularly of dramatic action, is something continuously latent in the order of words and is quite independent of direct influence. Rituals of human sacrifice were not common in Victorian England, but the instant Victorian drama becomes primitive and popular, as it does in *The Mikado,* back comes all Frazer's apparatus, the king's son, the mock sacrifice, the analogy with the Sacaea, and the rest of it. It comes back because it is still the primitive and popular way of holding an audience's attention, and the experienced dramatist knows it.

The prestige of documentary criticism, which deals entirely with sources and historical transmission, has misled archetypal critics into feeling that all ritual elements ought to be traced directly, like the lineage of royalty, as far back as a willing suspension of disbelief will allow. The vast chronological gaps resulting are sometimes bridged by a dubious conspiratorial theory of history involving secrets jealously guarded for centuries by esoteric cults. It is curious that when archetypal critics insist on continuous tradition they almost invariably produce some hypothesis of degeneration from a golden age lost in antiquity. Thus the prelude to Thomas Mann's Joseph series traces back several of our central myths to Atlantis, Atlantis being tolerable perhaps as an archetypal idea, but hardly as a historical one. When archetypal criticism revived in the 19th century with a vogue for sun myths, an attempt was made to ridicule it by proving that Napoleon was a sun myth. The ridicule is effective only against the historical distortion of the method. Archetypally, we turn Napoleon into a sun myth whenever we speak of the rise of his career, the zenith of his fame, or the eclipse of his fortunes.

Social and cultural history, which is anthropology in an extended sense, will always be a part of the context of criticism, and the more clearly the anthropological and the critical treatments of ritual are distinguished, the more beneficial their influence on each other will be. The same is true of the relation of psychology to criticism. Biography will always be a part of criticism, and the biographer will naturally be interested in his subject's poetry as a personal document, an interest that may take him into psychology. I am speaking here of the serious studies that are technically competent both in psychology and in criticism, which are aware how much guesswork is involved and how tentative all the conclusions must be. I am not speaking of the silly ones, which simply project the author's own erotica, in a rationalized clinical disguise, on his victim.

Such an approach is easiest and most rewarding with, say, Romantic poets, where the poet's own mental processes are often part of the theme. With a dramatist, who knows so well that "they who live to please must please to live," there is greater danger of making an unreal abstraction of the poet from his literary community. Suppose a critic finds that a certain pattern is repeated time and again in the plays of Shakespeare. If Shakespeare is unique or anomalous, or even exceptional, in using this pattern, the reason for his use of it may be at least partly psychological. But if we can find the same pattern in half a dozen of his contemporaries, we clearly have to allow for convention. And if we find it in a dozen dramatists of different ages and cultures, we have to allow for genre, for the structural requirements of drama itself.

A psychologist examining a poem will tend to see in it what he sees in the dream—a mixture of latent and manifest content. For the literary critic the manifest content of the poem is its form; hence, its latent content becomes simply its actual content or theme, Aristotle's *dianoia*. And in archetypal criticism the significant content of a poem is, we said, a dream. We seem to be going around in a circle, but not quite. For the critic, a problem appears that does not exist for a *purely* psychological analysis, the problem of communicable latent content, of intelligible dream. For the psychologist all dream symbols are private ones, interpreted by the personal life of the dreamer; for the critic there is no such thing as private symbolism, or, if there is, it is his job to make sure that it does not remain so.

This problem is already present in Freud's treatment of *Oedipus Rex* as a play that owes much of its power to the fact that it dramatizes the Oedipus complex. The dramatic and psychological elements can be linked without any reference to the personal life of Sophocles. The emphasis on impersonal content was developed by the Jungians, where the communicability of archetypes is accounted for by a theory of a collective unconscious—an unnecessary hypothesis in criticism, so far as I can judge. Now the poet, as distinct from the discursive writer, intends to write a poem, not to say something; hence he constructs a verbal pattern with, perhaps, millions of implications in it, of which he cannot be individually conscious. And what is true of the poet's intention is equally true of the audience's attention: their conscious awareness can take in only a very few details of the complex of response. This state of things enabled Tennyson, for instance, to be praised for the chastity of his language and read for his powerful erotic sensuousness. It also makes it possible for a contemporary critic to draw on the fullest resources of modern knowledge in explicating a work of art without any real fear of anachronism.

For instance, *Le Malade Imaginaire* is a play about a man who, in 17th century terms, including no doubt Molière's own terms, was not really sick but just thought he was. A modern critic may object that life is not so simple: that it is perfectly possible for a *malade imaginaire* to be a *malade veritable,* and that what is wrong with Argan is an unwillingness to see his children grow up, an infantile regression that his wife—his second wife, incidentally—shows that she understands completely by coddling him and murmuring such phrases as "pauvre petit fils." Such a critic would find the clue to Argan's whole behavior in his unguarded remark after the scene with the little girl Louison (the erotic nature of which the critic would also notice): "Il n'y a plus d'enfants." Such a reading, whether right or wrong, keeps entirely to Molière's text and has nothing to do with Molière himself.

Nor does it confine itself simply to the meaning of the play; it throws light on its narrative structure as well. The play is generically a comedy; it must therefore end happily; Argan must therefore be brought to see some reason; his wife, whose dramatic function it is to keep him within his obsession, must therefore be exposed as inimical to him. The movement of the play is exactly as logical and coherent as its total meaning, for the reason that they are the same thing, just as a piece of music is the same whether we listen to its performance or study its score. But, archetypally, the plot is a ritual moving through a scapegoat rejection to the prospect of marriage, which is the normal end of comedy, and the theme is a dream-pattern of irrational desire in conflict with reality. The archetypal is only one of many possible critical approaches, and in the case of a highly civilized comedy of 17th century France it may seem a somewhat peripheral one. But it gives us an insight into the structural principles of literature that we can get in no other way, as well as a clearer understanding of literature as a technique of communication.

KINESICS AND COMMUNICATION

Ray L. Birdwhistell

Kinesics is the study of the visual aspects of non-verbal, inter-personal communication. It is divided into three units: *Pre-kinesics* deals with physiological, pre-communicational aspects of body motion. *Micro-kinesics* is concerned with the derivation of kines (least particles of isolatable body-motion) into manageable morphological classes. And *social kinesics* is concerned with these morphological constructs as they relate to communication.

Pre-kinesics

Present research in kinesics assumes that visually perceptible body shifts, whose variations have been repetitively observed and are subject to systematization, are learned. This assumption does not preclude consideration of physiological influence. Generalizations about individual variations of velocity and intensity must await more definitive neuromuscular and endocrine research. But failure to keep pre-kinesics separate from micro-kinesics and social kinesics leads to reductionism. In the early stages of investigation, important data were overlooked by being dumped into the wastepaper baskets of "an itch," "weariness," "muscular relaxation," "tonus," and the like. But such stimuli to body movement are often, if not usually, dependent upon the context of the act and its social definition. To "scratch," to "shift," to "stretch," to "relax," and to "tense" are but a few of many apparently simple physiological reactions that are socially defined and controlled. To equivocate by calling them psychosomatic is to sacrifice experimental clarity for interdisciplinary fellowship.

In this discussion I shall use the closing and opening of the lids of one eye for illustration. This example contains much be-havior that is non-significant (at the present) to kinesiological research. For instance, a high-speed camera records almost a thousand positions of the lid in closing and opening. A graph derived from such a film strip shows rests, reverses, and velocity shifts that are imperceptible to the unassisted eye. Any society "selects" but a portion of this range for interactional definition.

The least isolated particle we call a *kine*. Members of a group use only certain of the discriminated range of kines for social interaction.

Micro-kinesics

Micro-kinesics deals with the systematization of kines with meaning into manageable classes. In a series of tests, five young nurses reported they could discriminate eleven positions of lid closure (eleven kines with discriminational meaning). All agreed that only four "meant" anything (four kines with differential meaning). Retesting of the nurses revealed that the latter were not precise positions but ranges of positions, which the nurses reported as "open-eyed," "droopy-lidded," "squinting," and "eyes squeezed tight," all of which they distinguished from just "open" and "closed."

Consequent to this research, it was found that only one of the five nurses could reproduce more than five of the twenty-three positions that they recognized to have differential meaning. Using a male control group of college students of comparable age, it was established that all could reproduce at least ten, with an average of fifteen. One extremely versatile young man produced thirty-five kines and easily got the twenty-three with differential meaning. Significantly, far less sex difference was noted in the ability of our Japanese and German informants. (This may be related to the small number of informants in the non-American groupings.) From this experiment, alone, we feel we have iso-lated significant recognition and reproduction differences within the informant range and between sexes. Just as we have a larger reading and hearing vocabulary than we do a speaking one, so we may have a larger viewing than acting list. Parenthetically, only morphological research has given us any feeling of security in describing any particular motion as *idiokinesic*.

To return to our methodological procedure: As soon as it was discovered that the variation of one or the other of the kines in a given area in the composite changed the differential meaning of the composite, we described the abstracted combination as a kinemorph. For example, "droopy-lidded," combined with "bilaterally raised, median portion depressed brows," has an evident differential meaning from "droopy-lidded" combined with a "low unilateral brow lift."

The discovery that the variation of *either* brow or lids may vary the differential meaning of the kinemorph relieves us from the over-easy temptation of indulging in discussion concerning modifiers and subjects or predicators. Nevertheless, I have a hunch that cross-cultural research is going to lead to the development of kinesic syntax. Present research seems to indicate that in middle-majority American culture circum-eye movement takes priority in definition of situation over movement of the hands, the ,arms, the trunk, and even over the head. This becomes apparent when we compare such data with that derived from Southern European and Southeast Asian informants.

Let me illustrate several of these points with an excerpt from an experiment:

Left eye closed; right open
Left orbital margin squinted
Mouth held in "normal"
Tip of nose depressed (bunnynose)
   (This projection held for no more than five seconds. Retest with shorter duration.)

Right eye closed; left open
Left orbital margin squinted
Mouth held in "normal"
Tip of nose depressed (bunnynose)
Informant's remark: "They look different, but they wouldn't mean anything different."
Tentative analysis: Shift from closing of right eye to left eye does not shift meaning. Leftness and rightness allokinic in this case. Use of unilateral squint unnoticed by informant.

Left eye closed; right open
Mouth held in "normal"
Tip of nose depressed
Neither orbital margin squinted
Informant's remark: "That's the same as the first."
Tentative analysis: Squint morphologically insignificant.

Left eye closed; right open
Left orbital margin squinted (or unsquinted)
Mouth drawn into pout
Tip of nose depressed
Informant's remark: "Well, that changes things."
Tentative analysis: Mouth position morphologically significant.

Here are two examples of recording situations. Both were taken in context, one on a bus, the second in a home. In only the second was there any direct information other than that supplied by the situation itself. Except insofar as there are regional cultural differences in the United States, these can be described as members of the common American culture. Mother and child spoke with a Tidewater, Virginia, accent. The hostess is a native of Cleveland, Ohio, resident in Washington since 1945; the guest is from a small Wisconsin town and is presently residing in Chicago. Both the hostess and the guest could probably be assigned an upper-middle-class position as measured by a Warner-type analysis. The bus route on which the bus event was recorded leads to a similar neighborhood. The way in which the mother and child were dressed was not consistent with the other riders, who disembarked, as did the observer, before the mother and child did. Both the hostess and her guest were in their late thirties. The child was about four, while his mother seemed to be about twenty-seven to thirty.

In Figures 1 and 2 stress and intonation are indicated above the pertinent text, using symbols provided in Trager and Smith's *Outline of English Structure;* voice-qualifiers, e.g., the drawl (⌒), are indicated by symbols developed by them. In a few places a phonemic transcription of the text is also provided. Kinesic symbols are given below the pertinent text, but are merely illustrated, not translated.

Social Kinesics

In this discussion I avoid the word "gesture," for gesture is restricted to those actions whose descriptions contain vocalized rationalizations by the actor or viewer. Research has revealed, however, that gestures are no more "meaningful" than other acts. The subjective, vocalized meanings attached to them do not necessarily supply us with insight into the meaning of the action, of which the gesture is an independent but deceptively visible aspect. Consider the variety of messages relayed by an action of which the "thumbed-nose" is the *explicit* focus. The delusory availability of gestures has provided the same handicap to the development of kinesics that formal grammar has to the under-

standing of linguistics. The most successful research in the field
of kinesics has come from the attempt to understand the relationship between visible and audible communication. New developments in linguistics make possible the organic relationship between such phonema; particularly intonation patterns, phrase
superfixes, and voice qualifiers. So intimate is this relationship
that the trained linguist-kinsiologist has at times been able to
describe many of the movements of a speaker from hearing a
recording or listening to a telephone conversation. Further, we
have found that an auditor may "hear" intonational shifts that
were not spoken but *moved* by the informant, and vice versa. Yet
these phenomena are not inseparable. Smith and Trager have
described as *meta-incongruent* the situation that occurs when the
subjective meaning carried by the words in an utterance is con-
tradicted by the intonation or voice-qualifiers used with it. A
comparable situation occurs when the utterance has one contextual
meaning and the accompanying action another. The utilization
of such data has evident value for interviewers. Meta-incongru-
ences are as important for those interested in "unconscious
behavior" as is the recognition that there occur kinesic "slips"
and "stuttering."

Of more interest perhaps to the non-linguist is the working
process of in-group conversation. As part of a study of an adoles-
cent clique, we paid particular attention to the "origin-response
ratio." Three of the nine boys in this group were, by word count,
heavy vocalizers. In fifteen recorded scenes (five scenes for each
of the three), they were responsible for from seventy-two to
ninety-three per cent *of the words* spoken. One of the three was
regarded by the group as a leader. (Incidentally, he originated
more conversations or new trends to conversation than any of
the other boys.) But the other recognized leader had one of the
lowest word count percentages of the group. He originated, by
our count, at a median rate, but he spoke only about sixteen per
cent of the words. His leadership seemed to be a kinesic one.

Compared with the other boys, he engaged in few unrelated
acts, that is, acts not traceably related to the interactional chain.
(These "unrelated acts" appear to be abortive efforts to originate
action; they seem related to similar behavior in smaller children,

1. This situation was observed on a street at about 2:30 P.M., April 14. The little boy was seated next to the window. He seemed tired of looking out of the window, and, after surveying all of the car ads and the passengers, he leaned toward his mother and pulled at her sleeve, pouted and vigorously kicked his legs.

2. His mother had been sitting erectly in her seat, her packages on her lap, and her hands lightly clasped around the packages. She was apparently "lost in thought."

3. When the boy's initial appeal failed to gain the mother's attention, he began to jerk at her sleeve again, each jerk apparently stressing his vocalization.

4. The mother turned and looked at him, "shushed" him, and placed her right hand firmly across his thighs.

5. The boy protested audibly, clenched both fists, pulled them with stress against his chest. At the same time he drew his legs up against the restraint of his mother's hand. His mouth was drawn down and his upper face was pulled into a tight frown.

6. The mother withdrew her hand from his lap and resettled in her former position with her hands clasped around the packages.

7. The boy grasped her upper arm tightly, continued to frown. When no immediate response was forthcoming, he turned and thrust both knees into the lateral aspect of her left thigh.

8. She looked at him, leaned toward him, and slapped him across the anterior portion of his upper legs.

9. He began to jerk his clenched fists up and down, vigorously nodding between each inferior-superior movement of his fists.

10. She turned, frowning, and with her mouth pursed, she spoke to him through her teeth. Suddenly she looked around, noted that the other passengers were watching, and forced a square smile. At the same time that she finished speaking, she reached her right hand in under her left arm and squeezed the boy's arm. He sat quietly.

⌒3/2 1⌒ 3/2|2 ∧   ∧   ⌒3/ + \1 # ⌒
1. Child: Mama.   I gotta go to the bathroom.
(mo) ⚲⟊ o o L35⊣ ⌒ ∧∧ ⌐˙˙¨˙¨ ˙¨˙ ¨˙ 2
          m8ther's sleeve   x

2. Mother:
          T ̈⊕ ⊕ ̈ 18XX1 ∧m∧ 3-3-3

      ⌒2/3 # ⌒2 ∧   ∧   3/1#
3. Child: Mama. Donnie's gotta go.
          R35⊣   R35⊣   R35⊣R35⊣R35⊣
          mo. r. sleeve

      ⌒2/ 1# ⌒
4. Mother: Sh-sh.
          ⚲ ⚲ R5 across child's lap - firm through 5

      1∪+⌒4 1# ⌒
5. Child: But mama.
          XX41 ⫯⫯ ⦚⦚

        ⌒ 3/ 1# ⌒ (o openness; ⩔over-softness)
6. Mother: ⩔ Later. ⩔
          18XX1 o o

      ⌒3/ 3 /1 / 1⌒(∧over-loudness; ≈whine)
7. Child: ≋ mah⟨ mah ≈
          R5 >⫯< ∧∧ zz against mother's thigh
          mother's arm

        ≋ 3/1# ≋ •   (?rasp)
8. Mother: ? Wait. ?
          ⚲ ⚲ ⚲ R14⊣ against child's thighs

      1∪+⌒3   1#⌒ 4/ 2/⌒ 4máh4/1máh# ⌒
9. Child: ˌˌOh mama. mama. ≋ mama.   ≋≋
          >∅ ∅<XX41↑ ┌──H ↓ ↑   ↓   ↑   H
                              ↓

      ≋3 / \1#≋⩔2/ |3   3# ⩔
10. Mother: ? Shut up.? ° Will yuh. o
          >⦚< ⇄ ⚲⚲ ⊙⊙ L35 child's l. u. arm
          ⩔   h   behind own r. arm

                    Figure 1

Guest of honor forty-five minutes late. Three couples waiting, plus host and hostess. Host had arranged guest list for function.

1. As the hostess opened the door to admit her guest, she smiled a closed-toothed smile. As she began speaking she drew her hands, drawn into loose fists, up between her breasts. Opening her eyes very wide, she then closed them slowly and held them closed for several words. As she began to speak she dropped her head to one side and then moved it toward the guest in a slow sweep. She then pursed her lips momentarily before continuing to speak, indicating that he should enter.

2. He looked at her fixedly, shook his head, and spread his arms with his hands held open. He then began to shuffle his feet and raised one hand, turning it slightly outward. He nodded, raised his other hand, and turned it palm-side up as he continued his vocalization. Then he dropped both hands and held them, palms forward, to the side and away from his thighs. He continued his shuffling.

3. She smiled at him, lips pulled back from clenched teeth. Then, as she indicated where he should put his coat, she dropped her face momentarily into an expressionless pose. She smiled toothily again, clucked and slowly shut, opened, and shut her eyes again as she pointed to the guest with her lips. She then swept her head from one side to the other. As she said the word "all" she moved her head in a sweep up and drown from one side to the other, shut her eyes slowly again, pursed her lips, and grasped the guest's lapel.

4. The guest hunched his shoulders, which pulled his lapel out of the hostess' grasp. He held his coat with both hands, frowned, and then blinked rapidly as he slipped the coat off. He continued to hold tightly to his coat.

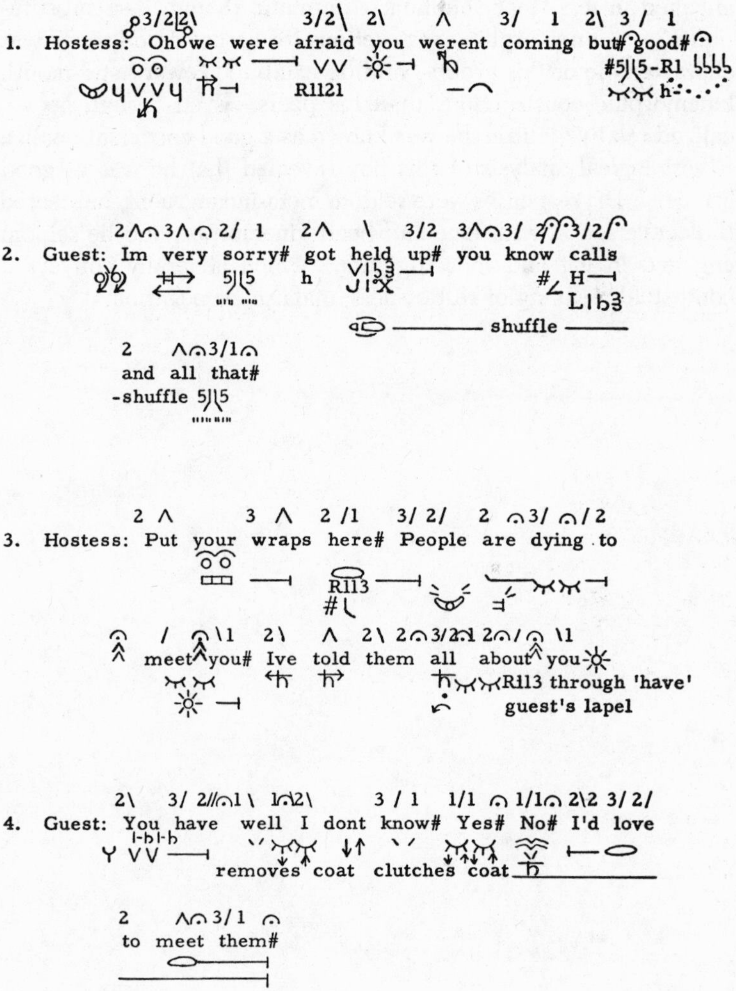

1. Hostess: Oh we were afraid you werent coming but# good#

2. Guest: Im very sorry# got held up# you know calls

   and all that#
   -shuffle

3. Hostess: Put your wraps here# People are dying to

   meet you# Ive told them all about you
   R113 through 'have'
   guest's lapel

4. Guest: You have well I dont know# Yes# No# I'd love

   removes coat clutches coat

   to meet them#

Figure 2

except that older children more frequently realize when the group is not responsive.) Compared with the adults in the neighborhood, he was kinesically more "mature" than the other boys. He engaged in less "foot shuffling," "dramatic thought"—a substitution (?) of kinemorphic constructions for verbal descriptions was characteristic of this group—and he exhibited fewer hand-mouth kinemorphic constructions than his peers. Even though he vocalized relatively little, he was known as a good conversationalist. Kinesiological analysis of this boy revealed that he was a "good listener." His responses were seldom meta-incongruent, he steered the conversation with face and head kinemorphs, and he seldom engaged in leg and foot "jiggling," which generally conveys a contextual meaning of restlessness, malaise, or negation.

ACOUSTIC SPACE

Edmund Carpenter and Marshall McLuhan

We often have difficulty in understanding a purely verbal notion. In *Alice in Wonderland:*

"'. . . the patriotic archbishop of Canterbury, found it advisable——'"
"Found *what?*" said the Duck.
"Found *it,*" the Mouse replied rather crossly: "of course you know what 'it' means."
"I know what 'it' means well enough, when *I* find a thing," said the Duck: "it's generally a frog or a worm. The question is, what did the archbishop find?"

We feel happier when *it* is visible; then it's oriented in a way we understand. For, in our workaday world, space is conceived in terms of that which separates visible objects. "Empty space" suggests a field in which there is nothing *to see*. We refer to a gasoline drum filled with pungent fumes or to a tundra swept by howling gales as "empty" because nothing is visible in either case.

Not all cultures think this way. In many preliterate cultures the binding power of oral tradition is so strong that the eye is subservient to the ear. In the beginning was the Word: a spoken word, not the visual one of literate man. Among the Eskimo, there is no silent sculpture. Idols are unknown; instead, deities are masked dancers who *speak* and *sing*. When the mask speaks it contains meaning and value; silent, static—illustrated in a book or hung in a museum—it is empty of value.

In our society, however, to be real, a thing must be visible, and preferably constant. We trust the eye, not the ear. Not since Aristotle assured his *readers* that the sense of sight was "above all others" the one to be trusted, have we accorded to sound a primary role. "Seeing is believing." "Believe half of what you see and nothing of what you hear." "The eyes of the Lord preserve knowledge, and he over-throweth the words of the transgressor." [Proverbs 22:12]. Truth, we think, must be observed by the "eye," then judged by the "I." Mysticism, intuition, are bad words among scientists. Most of our thinking is done in terms of *visual* models, even when an auditory one might prove more efficient. We employ spatial metaphor even for such psychological states as tendency, duration, intensity. We say "thereafter," not the more logical "thenafter"; "always" means "at all times"; "before" means etymologically "in front of"; we even speak of a "space" or an "interval" of time.

To the Eskimo, truth is given through oral tradition, mysticism, intuition, all cognition, not simply by observation and measurement of physical phenomena. To them, the ocularly visible apparition is not nearly as common as the purely auditory one; *hearer* would be a better term than *seer* for their holy men.

Now, every normal person, regardless of culture, spends the greater part of his waking activity in a visual world of three dimensions. If he thinks about the matter at all, he is inclined to conclude that this is the way, the only way, the world is made. It is therefore worth recalling that the child must *learn* to see the world as we know it. At or shortly after birth, his eyes are as perfectly developed a camera mechanism as they will ever be. In a sense they are too perfect and too mechanical, since they present him with a world in which everything is inverted, double, laterally reversed, and devoid of depth. In the course of time, by a tremendous tour de force of learning, he turns the world right side up, achieves binocular fusion, and reverses the lateral field so that he now sees his father as one person, erect, whole, and bilaterally oriented.

At the same time his growing capacity for movement leads him to explore this visual panorama tactually and kinesthetically. This activity is the basis of the development of the dominant characteristic of visual experience: depth. Without motor movement and its attendant kinesthesis, it is hard, if not impossible, to believe that depth perception would develop at all. Imagine a child incapable of motion from birth: that child would live in the two-dimensional world of its own retinae. No identifiable person or object, as such, could emerge for him, since, as his mother approached, she would appear as several different people of progressively greater size. Nor could such a child develop an awareness of himself. Even the congenitally blind child is not so handicapped: he has auditory space in which to function unimpaired by the hopeless visual conflicts of the hypothetical child, and, more importantly, he can explore this auditory world tactually while in motion. In other words, the chief characteristic of visual space—depth—is not primarily derived from visual experience at all, but comes rather from locomotion and its attendant kinesthesis.

We suppress or ignore much of the world as visually given in order to locate and identify *objects* in three dimensions. It is the objects which compel our attention and orient our behavior; space becomes merely that which must be traversed in getting to or from them. It exists between them, but they define it. Without them you have empty space. Most people feel an obscure gratitude to Einstein because he is said to have demonstrated that "infinite" space has a boundary of some kind. The gratitude flows, not because anyone understands how this can be, but because it restores to visual space one of its essential elements.

The essential feature of sound, however, is not its location, but that it *be*, that it fill space. We say "the night shall be filled with music," just as the air is filled with fragrance; locality is irrelevant. The concert-goer closes his eyes.

Auditory space has no point of favored focus. It's a sphere without fixed boundaries, space made by the thing itself, not space containing the thing. It is not pictorial space, boxed in, but dynamic, always in flux, creating its own dimensions moment by moment. It has no fixed boundaries; it is indifferent to background. The eye focuses, pinpoints, abstracts, locating each object in physical space, against a background; the ear, however, favors sound from any direction. We hear equally well from right or left, front or back, above or below. If we lie down, it makes no difference, whereas in visual space the entire spectacle is altered. We can shut out the visual field by simply closing our eyes, but we are always triggered to respond to sound.

Audition has boundaries only in terms of upper and lower thresholds. We hear waves produced by double vibration cycles of about 16 cycles per second up to about 20,000 per second. The amount of energy needed to produce an auditory sensation is so small that, were the ears just slightly more sensitive, we could hear molecules of air crashing into each other, provided, of course, we could learn to ignore the continuous Niagara of sound such ears would detect in the circulation of blood!

Auditory space has no boundaries in the visual sense. The distance a sound can be heard is dictated more by its intensity than by the capacity of the ear. We might compare this to looking at a star, where visual sensation, transcending the vanishing point, is achieved, but at the sacrifice of the precise framework we call visual space. There is nothing in auditory space corresponding to the vanishing point in visual perspective. One can, with practice, learn to locate many objects by sound, but this can be done so much better by vision that few of us bother. We continue to be amazed at the "psychic" powers of the blind, who establish direction and orientation by translating auditory-tactual clues into the visual knowledge they once had, an orientation infinitely more difficult for the congenitally blind.

In general, auditory space lacks the precision of visual orientation. It is easy, of course, to determine whether a sound comes from the right or left, because the width of the head makes it inevitable that the ears be stimulated by slightly different phases of the wave (a difference of 16/10,000 of a second can be detected). But it is impossible, while blindfolded, to judge accurately whether a neutral buzzer, at a constant distance, is directly before or behind one and, similarly, whether directly overhead or underfoot.

The universe is the potential map of auditory space. We are not Argus-eyed, but we are Argus-eared. We hear instantly anything from any direction and at any distance, within very wide limits. Our first response to such sensation is to move head and body to train our eyes on the source of the sound. Thus the two sense avenues coordinate as a team, each supplying an essential element for survival that the other lacks. Whereas the eyes are bounded, directed, and limited to considerably less than half the visible world at any given moment, the ears are all encompassing, constantly alert to any sound originating in their boundless sphere.

The ear is closely affiliated with man's emotional life, originally in terms of survival. The "sudden loud sound" that Watson thought produced an instinctive (unlearned) fear response in the infant still compels our quick (conditioned) fear response when perceived as, say, an automobile horn. It's the ambulance siren, not the blinker, that first warns us. Of what use would it be for a taxi driver to wave a flag or resort to any other visual equivalent for a warning? The onrushing cab itself is sufficient warning—if you happen to be looking that way! The dimensionless space of auditory sensation is the only hope in this circumstance; precisely because it is directionless, any sudden sound, from any quarter, will be attended to instantly.

Not all sounds are sudden, and not all are fear-producing. Auditory space has the capacity to elicit the gamut of emotions from us, from the marching song to opera. It can be filled with sound that has no "object," such as the eye demands. It need not be representational, but can speak, as it were, directly to emotion. Music can, of course, be visually evocative, as program music is, or it can be made to subserve the ends of visual presentation, as in the case of tin-pan alley tunes invented or stolen to fit lyrics. But there is no demand that music do either.

Poets have long used the word as incantation, evoking the visual image by magical acoustic stress. Preliterate man was conscious of this power of the auditory to make present the absent thing. Writing annulled this magic because it was a rival magical means of making present the absent sound. Radio restored it. In fact, in evoking the visual image, radio is sometimes more effective than sight itself. The squeaking door in *Inner Sanctum* was far more terrifying over radio than that same door seen and heard on television, because the visual image that sound evokes comes from the imagination.

This interplay between sense perceptions creates a redundancy, where, even if one element of a pattern is omitted, it is nevertheless implied. We feel, hear, and see "flaming, crackling red." Leave out "red," and it's still there; green neither flames nor crackles. In *The Eve of St. Agnes*, Keats describes how objects feel, taste, sound, and smell:

> . . . her vespers done,
> Of all its wreathed pearls her hair she frees;
> Unclasps her warmed jewels one by one;
> Loosens her fragrant boddice; by degrees
> Her rich attire creeps rustling to her knees. . . .

Elsewhere he describes fruit in terms of smell, taste, touch, even sound, and thus we experience the fruit; he uses lots of *l*'s and *o*'s and *u*'s; the mouth drips with honey as it forms these sounds.

This sort of interplay creates a dynamic process—being, alive, the ritual drama—particularly in primitive societies where the association of elements in such patterns is especially strong. Much of the intellectual excitement of 5th century Athens related to the discovery of the visual world and the translation of oral tradition into written and visual modes (probably the new role of the eye was as exciting to the Greeks as television is to us). The medieval world tried to channel the acoustic via Gregorian and liturgical chants, but it expanded into the visual world, and the resulting bulge or usurpation probably had much to do with the creation of "perspective" painting. For pure visual space is flat, about 180 degrees, while pure acoustic space is spherical. Perspective translated into visual terms the depths of acoustic space. The unscrambling of this mélange occurred via the photograph, which freed painters to return to flat space. Today we are experiencing the emotional and intellectual jag resulting from the rapid translation of varied visual and auditory media into one another's modalities.

SPACE CONCEPTION IN PREHISTORIC ART

S. Giedion

The problem of space conception is everywhere under discussion. Scholars ask themselves, for example, "What things have changed and what have remained unchanged in human nature throughout the course of human history? What is it that separates us from other periods? What is it that, after having been suppressed and driven into the unconscious for long periods of time, is now reappearing in the imagination of contemporary artists?"

This question of the continuity of human experience has interested me deeply for several years, especially in connection with the earliest beginnings of art (in prehistory) and of architecture (in Egypt and Sumer). I soon discovered that the existing photographic reproductions of primeval art were quite insufficient for the demands of modern art history. I therefore made several visits myself to the caverns in France and Spain, at first accompanied by Hugo P. Herdeg, one of the best Swiss photographers, then with both him and Achille Weider, then, since Herdeg's untimely death two years ago, with Weider alone. Together we accumulated the necessary photographs, which of course I selected carefully so that they should bring out those aspects that I consider relate to our immediate problems. Anyone who has ever attempted to work for eight or nine hours a day in these caverns will understand the difficulties we experienced in taking these pictures, which included some that had, up till then, proved impossible to photograph.

However, I was not just hunting for photographs. I was, above all, striving to come to a closer understanding of that fundamental human experience that goes by the name "art."

I have no doubt that this article on "space conception in

71

prehistoric art" will meet with opposition, for it is in direct contrast to the prevailing view that in prehistory "the single form is simply set off against chaos."

It is my belief that art cannot exist without a relation to the space around it—a space conception. The work of contemporary artists—for example, the structure of some of the works of Kandinsky and Klee—has shown us that prehistoric art is not necessarily chaotic. The art historian humbly accepts their silent lesson.

Prehistory is the pre-architectonic state of human development. As soon as architecture was evolved in Egypt and Sumer, and became predominant over sculptures and paintings, a new space conception was developed, which, with many variations, existed until the building of the Pantheon in Rome. From that time on a new phase came about—another space conception—which lasted until the 19th century. A third architectural space conception set in around the turn of the 20th century.

Intangibility of Space

It is possible to give physical limits to space, but by its nature space is limitless and intangible. Space dissolves in darkness and evaporates in infinity.

Means are necessary for space to become visible: it must acquire form and boundaries, either from nature or by the hand of man. All else is relative to this. Space is intangible, yet space can be perceived.

What constitutes this perception of space?

To confine emptiness within such dimensions that a form is created that elicits an immediate emotional response requires a complex set of conditions. The elucidation of the process by which an impression of inarticulate words is transformed into an emotional experience moves far away from logical reasoning.

What is it that happens?

In the realm of architecture, space is experienced by means of observation, in which the senses of sight and touch are interlocked. In the first instance this is a simple statement of fact. But through the relations of the most diverse elements and the degree of their emphasis—straight or curving lines, planes, structures, massivity, proportions, forms of all kinds—a matter of simple physical observation can be transposed to another sphere. These diverse elements are seen suddenly as a single entity, as a oneness, imbued with spiritual qualities. This transformation of a simple physical fact into an emotional experience derives from a higher level of our faculty of abstraction. Before discussing this it is necessary to go briefly into the beginnings of the perception of space and its early supremacy.

The Nature of Space Conception

The first observable fact about space is its emptiness—an emptiness through which things move or in which things stand. The human demiurge—the almost godlike human compulsion to invent new things and to give a spiritual quality to impressions of the senses—also operates in connection with space. Man takes cognizance of the emptiness that girdles him and gives it a psychic form and expression.

The effect of this transfiguration, which lifts space into the realm of the emotions, is termed space conception. This space conception portrays man's relations with his environment.

Space conception is a psychic recording of the realities that confront him. The world that lies about him becomes transformed. He thus realizes, so to speak, his urge to come to terms with it, to give a graphic expression of his position toward it.

In their first Manifesto of 1924, the Surrealists speak of an "*Automatisme psychique pur* par lequel on se propose d'exprimer, soit verbalement, soit par écrit, soit de toute autre manière, le fonctionnement réel de la pensée. Dictée de la pensée, on l'absence de toute contrôle exercé par la raison." [1] A space conception is just such an automatic physic recording in the realm of the visible environment. It develops instinctively, usually remaining unknown to its authors. It is just because of its unconscious and, so to speak, compulsive manifestation that a space conception provides such an insight into the attitude of a period to the cosmos, to man, and to eternal values.

[1] André Breton, *Manifeste de Surréalisme*, Paris, 1924, p. 42.

This attitude toward space changes continuously, sometimes by small degrees, sometimes basically. As will appear later, there have been very few space conceptions in the whole development of man. Each covered long periods of time. Within each of these epochs, however, many variations and transitions have been built up; for relations with space are always in a state of suspension, and the transitions flow in and out of one another.

The Space Conception of Primeval Art

What is the space conception of primeval art?

If by space conception we mean the power of any period to transform a simple act of perception into an emotional experience, then we can say that no art exists that is not based on a relationship with space.

The space conception of a period is the graphic projection of its attitude toward the world. This holds true whether we consider Renaissance art, in which everything is dominated by the eye of the beholder—a space conception that is graphically depicted by the perspective projection of long, level vistas upon a plane surface; or Egyptian art, in which several different aspects of the same object are depicted upon horizontal and vertical planes undistorted and in their natural size; or in Neolithic art, in which geometric abstractions are left hovering in space.

At the base of the first two of these space conceptions lies a sense of order that has been rooted deep in our human nature for over 5000 years. This sense of order involves—at least ever since the times of Egypt and Sumer—the relation of everything that one sees to the vertical or the horizontal. Each of us carries in his brain a sort of secret balance that unconsciously impels us to weigh everything we see in relation to the horizontal and vertical. This ranges from the composition of a painting to the most ordinary of our everyday habits. We feel slightly uneasy when our knife and fork are not laid straight beside our plate at table or when the writing paper on our desk is not parallel to the blotter. However, this is not the only conception of order that can exist. There is another that is not dependent upon the vertical, and this occurs in primeval art.

The pictorial composition of prehistoric artists is not rational to our way of thinking. But they were nevertheless able to master the syntax of pictorial art.[2] It is simply that they had a different approach to art from the one to which we have become accustomed, ever since we accepted the dominance of the vertical and the horizontal, which—including their natural corollary, symmetry—have become so embedded in our consciousness that they seem to be an absolute condition of order.

This way of looking at things was unknown to prehistoric man, as indeed it still is to primitive peoples. Ambiguity, the existence of apparent contradictions and of the interweaving of events without regard to our sense of time (before and after) are the matters that find expression in primeval art.

What is it that differentiates the space conception of prehistory from that of the other periods? Are there any criteria that persisted throughout the whole period of prehistoric art?

It was almost by chance that I discovered how the prehistoric artist organized his composition and thus revealed his attitude toward space.

Not far from Les Eyzies lies the little museum of Laugerie Basse, situated directly under an overhanging curtain of rock. Laugerie Basse was one of the first sites excavated. The first discoverers of primeval art—a Frenchman and an Englishman, E. Lartet and H. Christy—conducted their excavations here in 1863 and reported their findings in their *Reliquiae Aquitanicae*.

In the little museum there was a triangular block of stone with incurving sides, which caught my eye because of its shape. I took it out into the sunshine. It then became apparent that on the upper part of the left face and tilting downward there was an engraved outline of a bull. Its hindquarters disappeared into the stone together with the extremities of its hind legs. The line of its back was, however, very firmly engraved with a sharp kink at the position of the shoulder blades. As is so often the

[2] Moritz Hoernes and Oswald Menghin, *Urgeschichte der bildenden Kunst in Europe*, Vienna, 1925, p. 127.

case in prehistoric works of art, the head was strongly molded. At first glance it appeared as though the animal were grazing on a slightly convex ledge, with his strongly emphasized forelegs resting on a lower level.

When I lifted up the stone to take it back, I turned it by chance round an angle of 180 degrees. This enabled me to see that the curve of the ledge composed the neck and the chest of another animal, which, in our way of looking at pictures, would be described as standing on its head. The stretched-out neck and head of this gazelle-like creature stood out clearly in the altered angle of light. The rest of its body was only roughly indicated. Apparently the animal was depicted in flight. An outstretched foreleg lay alongside the head of the bull, which, again due to the change of light, had disappeared—at least from our eyes. But the eyes of prehistoric man were free. He did not find it necessary to translate every composition into vertical parallels.

This carved block is certainly one of the less important works of the Magdalenian period, but through my chance turning of it I had seen the light make animals appear and disappear. This made me suddenly aware of the intentions of primeval art —of its principle of composition. It became clear to me that Paleolithic man looked at things and at space in a way different from that to which we have become accustomed.

Eskimos and Magdalenian Art

Some years later, when on a visit to Canada, I received additional confirmation of this from an anthropologist in the University of Toronto, Edmund Carpenter. Carpenter had lived for some time with the Aivilik Eskimos on the 20,000 square miles of Southampton Island north of Hudson Bay. In his essay "Eskimo Space Concepts" he examines the space concepts of the Aivilik Eskimos in relation to their sense of direction, their views of the universe, and above all their art.

The way of life of the Eskimo is, roughly speaking, similar to that of Magdalenian man in the Ice Age. The Eskimos are more "primitive" than the North American Indians, who show in their art that they have already become dominated by vertical and horizontal and the need to organize these lines of direction upon a plane surface.

If an Aivilik Eskimo is given a photograph the wrong way up, he doesn't find it necessary to twist it around. When Eskimo children cannot complete their drawing upon a sheet of paper, they draw the rest of it upon the other side. This is similar to the way the Eskimos compose their engravings on bone or walrus teeth. They have a "habit of scratching until a figure reaches the limits of the ivory, then turning the tusk over and completing the figure on the reverse side."

"In handling these cribbage boards," says Carpenter, "I found myself turning them first this way, then that, orienting each figure in relation to myself. The Aivilik do not do this. Carvers draw a number of figures each oriented—by our standards—in a different direction."

E. S. Carpenter kindly sent me the reproduction of a reindeer knife-handle from the Eskimo (Royal Ontario Museum, Toronto) which depicts a caribou in two characteristic positions: one on guard, the other grazing. If the handle is turned through 90 degrees the grazing animal becomes upright and watchful.

In publications on Eskimos by excellent ethnologists one frequently finds that the explorers gave a pencil and the flat surface of a sheet of paper to the Eskimos, asking them to reproduce their animals and their demons. The result is highly unattractive, with no emotional impact. The reason is that the two-dimensional material was not an adequate means of expression for them. What they needed for their imagination was a walrus-tusk with all its freedom. Since the time of their crossing of the Bering Strait from Asia around 1500 B.C., the Eskimos have held fast to their concept of space as their prehistoric heritage if they were not spoiled by Western influence.

A small object from *art mobilier* may remind us of prehistoric spontaneity in the use of planes and directions. On a *propulseur* (spear-thrower) from Mas d'Azil two protruding ends of a reindeer antler are used to carve two horses' heads facing in different directions. A third one, a skinless head, is turned upside-down, for us completely unexpectedly.

It is this manner of seeing things without any "relation to myself" that distinguishes primeval art from all later art. It is not disorder but a different form of order that is being followed —an order to which we, in our sophistication, have lost the key.

Caverns Are Not Architecture

The dwellings of prehistoric man were not located in the interior of caves. They sheltered under overhanging rocks, as in Laugerie Haute and Laugerie Basse (Dordogne, France), and in the mouth of caves, as at Altamira (Spain), or just nearby, as in Comparelles (Dordogne, France), where, along a low corridor, dark stains have been found near fissures in the rock, through which smoke could escape.

No traces of human dwellings have been found in the interior of the caverns. These were holy places in which, with the aid of magically potent pictures, the sacred rituals could be performed.

These caverns owed their existence to the forces of erosion, which often endowed them with fantastic formations. Sometimes surfaces had been polished smooth by sand and water. The heavy clay sank to the ground but also, in many cases, adhered to walls and ceilings. After the period of upheaval, drops of hard calcareous water from mountain streams filtered through the ceilings and gradually deposited translucent curtains over the walls or formed columns, which grew from the top down or from the ground up until after they met in the middle.

In some of the caverns where tourists are not permitted to enter and which have remained undisturbed throughout tens of thousands of years, dreamlike crystal growths arise from the ground—thickly clustered, white as snow, and fine as needles— as in the Tuc d'Audoubert (Pyrenees, France). These fantastic subterranean caverns undoubtedly breathe an air of marvel and mystery. But one must beware. These caverns, which are the containers of primeval art, have nothing to do with architecture.

Everyone is free to interpret the fantastic forms occurring in these caverns as cathedrals, banquet halls, galleries, chapels, or what have you, but actually these uninterrupted sequences of forms, sometimes sharply defined, sometimes utterly amorphous, have no connection whatever with architecture.

Vaults, so high that they are beyond the reach of the beam of light from one's lantern, alternate with tubelike passages, so low that one must crawl painfully along them, with sudden abysses, with great boulders, and with falls of rubble. Further, the caverns possess only an interior; they have no exterior. In all this they are quite different from the architecture later invented by man.

These caverns possess no space in our meaning of this word, for in them perpetual darkness reigns. The caverns are, spatially speaking, empty. This is well appreciated by anyone who has tried alone to find his way out from one of them. The weak beam of light from his torch is swallowed up by the absolute darkness around him, while rocky tunnels and crumbling slopes repeat themselves in every direction and re-echo his question: where is the outlet from this labyrinth?

Light and the Art of the Caverns

Nothing is more destructive of the true values of primeval art than the glare of electric light in this realm of eternal night.[3] Flares or small stone lamps burning animal fat, of which examples have been found, permit one to obtain only fragmentary glimpses of the colors and lines of the objects depicted. In such a soft, flickering light these take on an almost magical movement. The engraved lines, and even the colored surfaces, lose their intensity under a strong light and sometimes disappear altogether. Only a soft side-lighting—*lumière frisée*—can awaken their original strength. Only in this way can the fine veining of the drawings be seen unsmothered by their rough background.

Maybe enough has now been said to show that prehistoric man did not associate the caverns with architecture. In his view the caverns simply provided him with places that he could use for his magic arts. He selected these places with the utmost care.

[3] It is unfortunately often necessary to use flash bulbs when taking photographs in the caverns, but whenever at all possible we always used softer lights with reflectors.

Some were perhaps chosen because the rock formation seemed particularly suitable. But most were chosen because he believed them to possess special powers. There were no fixed rules.

However, one predisposition can be detected that recurs repeatedly. This is that prehistoric man did not consider the caverns as an edifice to be decorated: secret signs and figurations are placed in positions that are extremely difficult of access and at the uttermost end of the caves, where the walls narrow to a mere crack. In these cases it is clear that prehistoric man was more anxious to hide his artistic creations than to expose them. They came and went in the dim light of his flickering lamps. The tradition of secreting the most sacred manifestations in places accessible only to the initiated persisted in the Egyptian temples, where the statue of the god was concealed in a dark cell at the farthest extremity of the temple. No one but the king and the high priest had access to this place. What in prehistory was provided by nature has here become translated into architecture.

Once it has become clear that prehistoric man did not look upon the caverns as an architectural space, we can realize the freedom with which he was able to employ natural materials for his purposes, and the new concept of prehistoric space conception begins to emerge: the unfettered imaginative power with which prehistoric man handles surfaces and his attitude toward them.

Freedom of Approach to All Surfaces

The surfaces of the caverns and overhanging cliffs are sometimes flat and sometimes curved. They change continually in their form and in their direction, sometimes also in their color. This is particularly true of the limestone rocks and caverns of the Dordogne—that center of primeval art. Here the rock walls are as smoothly polished as though a glacier had passed over them. The surfaces are, however, never regular. The rock walls curve gently in every possible direction.

This multiformity of the surfaces, their infinite freedom of direction and perpetual change, is at the basis of all primeval art, which is closer than any other to nature but still knows how to preserve the essential individuality of human existence.

It would, despite everything, have been possible to select vertical and horizontal planes. But this was never done. None of the variously sloping surfaces receives any preference. To be chosen, a surface must possess some magical properties. In any case primeval art is not used to "decorate" a space in our way of thinking. In prehistory man was completely unfettered in the way in which he selected surfaces.

This is why we have to free ourselves as much as possible from the way of looking at things that has been part of our inheritance for thousands of years, if we wish to come near to an understanding of primeval art. The lines and orientation of a picture have no relation to the horizontal or vertical; nor is the selection of the surface dependent upon its angle of inclination. Whether the structure and shape of the surface be smooth, curved, or cracked, one can always see an ability to use it to the full.

The Pech-Merle Ceiling

Only a few instances can be noted here. On the damp, clay ceiling of the so-called Salle des Hiéroglyphes in the cavern of Pech-Merle, which measures about 10 by 4 meters, generation after generation in Aurignacian times drew with their fingers the outlines of supplicatory figures, superimposing them one upon the other: mammoths, bird-headed goddesses, and some fragments of other beings. These were carefully copied and deciphered by their discoverer Abbé Lemozi. He worked lying upon his back in a most hazardous situation, upon the smooth and slippery rocks that lay under the ceiling and sloped away into nothingness. The designs upon this ceiling, which date from the beginnings of art, are suspended above a void. Here there can have been no question of decorating a space.

Many millennia later, the same phenomenon appears upon the ceiling of the cavern of Altamira, which represents the apex of Magdalenian art. This rock vault is only five feet from the ground, so it is impossible to stand upright beneath it. A pathway has therefore been dug out for visitors to walk along. Over this low vault spread the famous frescoes with their animals and gigantic symbols, which on one side merge into the earth. To get a good view of this ceiling one must lie stretched out upon the original level of the floor. Even then it is not possible for the eye to take in the structure of the entire composition at one glance. It was not created for the public nor to decorate a space: it is magic that exists for itself.

Neither the slightly curved Pech-Merle ceiling, from the earliest period, nor the Altamira ceiling, from the period of highest artistic knowledge in prehistory, spans any architectural space. Each exists for itself alone, hovering independently over the hollow space below.

The Lascaux Gallery

Curved and winding surfaces are handled in a similar way. Sometimes naturally formed arches and passages take on such regular shapes that they appear to be the work of human hands. The domelike vault and branching passages of Lascaux are like this. The ceilings are composed of very thick nonporous lime-stone. Through condensation they became entirely covered with tiny lime crystals, which provide a magnificently solid painting surface. The walls, on the other hand, are impossible to paint on, being made up of brittle rock with horizontal cracks.

The dome, with its frieze of gigantic animals, as well as the passage that leads almost axially from it (called, from its position, the *diverticule axial*) both show the manner of handling curved surfaces. The tunnel-like passage is particularly instructive. At first sight the semicircular vault of the near part of its roof, with its luminous colors and crystalline background, has almost the appearance of a gallery in an Italian baroque castle. Closer observation shows, however, that the same attitude has been adopted in painting this curving, concave surface, which stretches away into the distance, as was used in making the minute Magdalenian engravings upon rounded pieces of bone.

The red-brown primeval cattle, yellow and black horses, punc-
tuations, and other magical signs are all freely disposed at varying angles, and yet one cannot help realizing that there is a
general sense of composition. This can be instanced by the
dynamic organization of the tapering heads and necks of three
red-brown cattle. The rest of their bodies curve over the ceiling.
The group is joined by a yellow "Chinese" pony, drawn to quite
another scale, and a stream of other animals stretches away to
right and left.

This different way of looking at things is just what interests
us today: the way in which prehistoric man could grasp things
in their entirety without needing to organize them according to
a static viewpoint or to adjust them to the vertical. This is
brought out by the position given to a red bull in this sloping
passage. To our eyes he appears to be leaping over a chasm.

Probably Magdalenian man saw no leap and no abyss. He
simply saw a third animal who came to join the other two. This
follows the same principle of vision as was shown on the carved
triangular block of Laugerie Basse.

At the very end of the *diverticule axial* at Lascaux are a
number of horses. One of them "has fallen over backwards with
all four feet in the air." This horse, who has "tumbled over a
precipice," has been interpreted as evidence of an animal tragedy,
well known in Solutrean times, when herds of wild horses were
driven over cliffs. But here, too, it would seem that one should
be cautious about such naturalistic interpretations. It is probable
that the horse at Lascaux has no more fallen into an abyss than
the multicolored bison at Castillo is climbing vertically up a
stalacmite.

This bison can be found in the second chamber of the cavern
at Castillo, which lies a few hundred yards from La Pasiega.
The bold carving of his powerful loins strikes one immediately
on entering the hall because of the deep dent thus made in one
of the stalacmite columns, which distinguishes it from all the
others that surround it. A nearer view shows that some parts of
the animal—tail, flanks, the outline of the back and the belly—
"sont formés par un accident rocheaux," as was noted by Alcalde

del Rio, who discovered this cavern in 1903, and Abbé Breuil, who first described and illustrated it.[4]

Irregular Convex Surfaces: Castillo and Altamira

As is universally the case in primeval art, the eye of the Ice Age hunter discovers images of the animals he seeks in the structure of the rocks. The French describe this recognition of natural formations as "épouser les contours." A few lines, a little carving, or some color are enough to bring the animal into view.

In Altamira a Magdalenian artist was able to transform the hideous excrescences from the ceiling into bison—lying, falling, or standing—with a mastery of line and color hitherto unknown.

Several hundred years earlier, the slight carving of the vertical buffalo of Castillo gives evidence of the same principle: the power to handle irregular surfaces with complete freedom. Whether the animal appears in a vertical position or in any other position is quite irrelevant to the eye of prehistoric man.

In forming the Castillo bison, the artist proceeded from the natural shapes before him. He carved in the hind hoofs very precisely, just beneath the swelling flanks; he strengthened the natural outline of the hindquarters and the belly; and he added with a bit of black color the mane and the lower parts. The animal's small head, lightly sketched-in horns, and painted nose almost disappear into the rock. All emphasis was concentrated on the tension of his sinewy body.

Sloping Surfaces: the Bisons of Tuc d'Audoubert

Freedom of approach to all surfaces, regardless of horizontal or vertical direction, is a basic principle of primeval art. This is shown again in an unusual situation where the background for a work of art had first to be prepared—the case of the two bison modeled in high relief in the *sancta sanctorum* of the cavern of Tuc d'Audoubert. These bison were modeled upon an inclined

[4] H. Alcalde del Rio, Abbé Henri Breuil, R. Père Lorezo Sierra, *Les Cavernes de la Région Cantabrique (Espagne)*, Monaco, 1912, p. 149, plates 75 and 76.

plane. Their base is a block of rock fallen from the ceiling. In their almost inaccessible, but most carefully considered, situation at the farthest end of the cavern, these two animals have been molded upon the rock in the damp clay of the cavern. They could just as easily have been modeled in a vertical position, but they were not. The inclined plane heightens the impressiveness of this fertility rite and makes the mounting position of the male animal terrifyingly vivid. The very use of the inclined plane makes clear the freedom of approach of primeval art to the surface plane.

The question whether there was any feeling of composition and artistic sense of emphasis in the primeval period is here answered with a rare clarity.

First, there is a stream that flows into the cavern and then suddenly disappears under the ground. In the cavern of Tuc d'Audoubert itself one must climb through three levels before one reaches an entrance that bears the impress of feet of the Magdalenian period. These heel marks lead one to believe that this is a place similar to the *Salle des Hiéroglyphes* at Pech-Merle, with the bird-goddesses upon the ceiling. Finally, at the uttermost end of the cavern, beneath a high vaulted roof, the pair of bison have been placed upon a kind of altar. Their modeling is so strong that it emanates an extraordinary sense of space, although in fact their size is surprisingly small: the bull being 24½ inches long and the cow 23½ inches.

Summary

The distinguishing mark of the space conception of primeval art is the complete independence and freedom of its vision, which has never again been attained in later periods. In our sense there is no above and no below, no clear distinction of separateness from an intermingling, and also, certainly, no rules of proportional size. Gigantic animals of the Magdalenian era stand alongside tiny deer from Aurignacian times, as, for example, on the dome of Lascaux. Violent juxtaposition in size as well as in time is accepted as a matter of course. All is within the continual present, the perpetual interflow of today, yesterday, and tomorrow.

Every prehistoric work of art is a proof of this. Whenever possible previous designs are not destroyed, but the lines of both earlier and later works intermingle till they sometimes—but only to our eyes—appear inextricable. It was recognized quite early that this superimposition was not due to idle chance but to a deliberate reluctance to destroy the past. Peyrony and Capitan, who, in the early days of this century, explored the most important cavern of the Dordogne, even then pointed out:

Whenever one finds drawings of different periods superimposed upon one another, the last ones, though they bear no relation to the others, never destroy them more than is absolutely necessary for their own execution. The older drawings were never deliberately destroyed. On the contrary they were respected almost as though they were sacred.[5]

Primeval art was made by nomads. This being so, it is a matter for wonder that many of the caverns contain works ranging from the beginning to the end of prehistory—from the Aurignacian to the Azilian eras. This is a period far outside the range of our limited conception of time.

The Coming Change

History discloses that a space conception—man's attitude toward space—is maintained over long periods of time, which in other respects may show great changes. It is unfortunately not possible to develop this theme here or to give more than a very few indications of subsequent developments.

Primeval art never places objects in an immediate surrounding. Primeval art has no background. This is apparent in such large murals as the ceiling of Altamira as well as in the small ritual objects of *art mobilier*. This is inherent in the prehistoric conception of space: all linear directions have equal right and likewise all surfaces, whether they be regular or irregular. They can be tilted at any angle with the horizontal throughout the entire

[5] Capitan and Peyrony, *L'Humanité primitive dans la région des Eysies,* Paris, 1924, pp. 95–96.

360 degree range. To the eye of primeval man, animals that to us appear to be standing on their heads, do not appear inverted to him because they exist, as it were, in space free from the forces of gravity. Primeval art has no background.

The rise of the high civilization of Sumer and Egypt changed all this. The relation to an unlimited number of directions became replaced by the relation to a single direction: the vertical. The horizontal is only its natural by-product, as is the 90 degree angle they define. With the increasing dominance of the vertical as the ruling principle, the axis and bilateral symmetry appear throughout the composition of the reliefs, the sculpture, and the emerging architecture.

In the second volume of a forthcoming study, we will trace this development throughout the formative period of Egyptian art, when all directions became related to the vertical line and all surfaces became subordinated to the vertical plane, including all the parts of the human body. Although these changes are mentioned here only in order to contrast them with prehistoric freedom, there is in one respect a certain link to prehistoric representation: all objects are projected upon a flat plane which does not allow the actual distortions of perspective as they appear to the natural eye. The Egyptian eye immediately translated these flattened figures into three dimensions with the same ease with which the primeval eye adjusted animals in any conceivable position.

Two examples will suffice: the first is a primitive shrine to the goddess *Neith* of the early dynastic period, which is depicted in such a way that the enclosing walls, as well as the court, are flattened out into one vertical plane.[6] It is difficult for our eyes to adjust to this convention and to see the form as the early Egyptians saw it. This way of conceiving and representing objects never changed throughout ancient Egyptian art. The second example is a wall painting from the middle of the 15th century B.C. which demonstrates what great charm this, so to say, mathematical projection could attain. It is a wall painting in Thebes, from the tomb of *Rekh-nu Re* (copy in tempera in the Museum of Modern Art, New York). A pool is represented with two servants drawing water. As in all Egyptian art, the depth of the

---

[6] A. Badawy, *History of Egyptian Architecture,* Cairo, 1954, figure 22.

water is indicated by vertical zig-zag lines. The trees which surround the pool are laid down horizontally. The two servants draw water in well-shaped vessels. Their movements are free and elegant, although their bodies are rigidly related at right angles to each other.

Prehistoric Space Conception and Contemporary Art

Abstraction, transparency, and symbolization are constituent elements of prehistoric and contemporary art. The space in which they evolve has many things in common. Differences exist, but this is not the occasion to go into them. At the moment only their inner relationship is what interests us. Their space is a space without background, a universal space. We are indebted to artists like Kandinsky and Klee for slowly being able to grasp the space conception of primeval art. They have opened our eyes to the picture's organization, which is not exclusively dependent on the vertical. In Kandinsky's early work—*e.g., The White Edge* (Guggenheim Museum, New York, 1913)—we find a passion to exploit the newly gained freedom of lines and color set in sideral space. Paul Klee followed the same path, but in his own way. In one of his popular and most frequently reproduced paintings— *The Landscape with Yellow Birds* (Kunstmuseum, Basel)—the birds are sitting on fantastic plants, which defy botanical definition. On the upper rim of the picture one of the yellow birds is represented upside-down, indicating the spatial fluidity. One is reminded of underwater landscapes, where the body may move in all directions, unhindered by gravity. Developed even further is the cosmic atmosphere in the far less known *Ad Marginem* (1930). A planet hovers in the middle of a greenish undetermined background. Fantastic figurations grow along the margin. Plants, animals, eyes are forms in *status nascendi,* polyvalent in their significance. Like primeval hybrid figures, they too cannot be confined to a definite zoological species. Here and there a calligraphically precise letter is inscribed in one of these forms, suddenly losing its everyday aspect and being re-transformed into a magic symbol from which it originated. From the upper rim, the naked stem of a plant is thrust down, and a bird with a long beak marches upside-down in a space without gravity. The forms reveal not even the remotest similarity with prehistoric motifs. Only the problem of constancy—as we understand it—comes to the fore, not in the sense of a rational, direct continuation, but rather as that property of the human mind which has been submerged for years in fathomless depths, suddenly reappearing on the surface. This happened in our time.

THE MOVING EYE

Jacqueline Tyrwhitt

Twenty-three miles from Agra in India, with its fabled Taj Mahal, lies Fatehpur Sikri, a dream city built in sandstone the colors of the dying sunset. One approaches Fatehpur Sikri in silence, for it has been deserted for over two hundred years, but immediately on entering the core of the city—the Mahal-i-Khas —the heart is uplifted, the eye entranced. One experiences a rare sensation of freedom and repose—an invitation to step forward buoyantly and, at the same time, to loiter luxuriously. Wherever the eye turns the view is held, but at every step it changes. A seemingly solid background wall of stone is later perceived as a transparent screen. But nowhere is there a fixed center: nowhere a point from which the observer can dominate the whole. Equally nowhere does he stand conspicuously removed from the center—a spectator in the wings. From the moment he steps within this urban core he becomes an intimate part of the scene, which does not impose itself upon him, but discloses itself gradually to him, at his own pace and according to his own pleasure.

The Mahal-i-Khas was the core of a city of perhaps fifty thousand people. It is a place somewhat larger than the Piazza San Marco in Venice and, like it, is framed by buildings and openings, as well as having buildings standing within it as objects, both dimensioning its own space and being set off by it. Despite un-Western details of architectural ornament, the contemporary visitor to Fatehpur Sikri is at once struck by the likeness of the spatial composition of these solids and voids in the Mahal-i-Khas to our modern Western thinking about the interplay of freedom and enclosure, transparency and repose.

Nothing in this deserted city of Fatehpur Sikri is fortuitous,

and none of the effects are due either to the accretions of time
or to its ravages. The city was built at one stroke by Akbar the
Magnificent around 1570 and was deserted, but not destroyed,
some twenty years later. Though many of the buildings themselves are very fine, the supreme quality of the Mahal-i-Khas lies
in its superb proportioning of space. Most of the buildings within
and around it are themselves symmetrical in their design, but
their spatial setting is never axial. While it is clear at first glance
that this is an ordered composition, one looks in vain for the key
to it in terms of Western academic art. This article is an attempt
to find that key.

It is very difficult for us to get away from the rules of the
accepted vision of our Western culture and to realize, even intellectually, that this is not the only way of looking at things. For
instance our eyes in the West have for five hundred years been
conditioned, even governed, by another intellectual approach:
the single viewpoint. This, though no more intellectual than the
acceptance of the dominance of the vertical, is more readily
grasped as an acquired characteristic of our vision. It is, however, peculiar to the Western world, where it followed the development of the science of optics: the study of the eye as an
inanimate piece of mechanism pinned down upon the board of
the scientist. The optical result was the development of linear
perspective: the single "vanishing point" and the penetration of
landscape by a single piercing eye—my eye, my dominating eye.
This created a revolution in our way of perceiving the objects
around us and in the rational organization of landscape—whether
rural or urban. The "view" came into being: the penetration of
infinity by means of a guided line—usually an avenue of trees
or a symmetrical street. With this came the "vista," the termina-
tion of the organized view by an object of interest, often the
elaborately symmetrical façade of a large building, that could
only be rightly beheld from a central point at some distance
from it. All other views were, consciously and unconsciously,
accepted as wrong: "This is the place to see it from."

For many it is extremely difficult, even uncomfortable, to
accept linear perspective as a conditioned form of vision, limited
and partial in its scope. "That is exactly the way it looks to me"

is the usual description of a good photograph, for the camera with its single fixed eye expresses linear perspective perfectly. But the rest of the world sees things quite differently.

A Chinese painting is always presented to a spectator whose eye roves along a scroll or up a vertical painting. For instance, in a typical vertical painting of mountain scenery, the spectator will first find himself looking slightly down upon a cottage or fisherman at the foot of the picture—his eye perhaps on the level with the branches of a nearby pine tree. Then he will notice the ascending mountain path, but by now his eye will have moved, and he will be scanning the scenery from a higher vantage point. After a bit his moving eye will light upon a high mountain meadow, or other resting place, and from there, from that viewpoint, he will look up to the inaccessible peaks, half hidden in cloud. The spectator does not see an instantaneous picture of the entire mountain scene through the peephole of an imaginary camera in the cockpit of a helicopter hovering in mid-air; he participates, through his moving eye, in the inter-relationship of man and mountain. Similarly, on the long scroll paintings, the eye moves slowly into the picture from the right, the scene always changing, always unfolding. Objects usually come toward the spectator rather than recede from him, for here the eye seldom pierces the landscape. The technique of drawing is a form of parallel perspective rather than linear perspective: the spectator usually being at an angle to the scene (rather than the focus of it) and parallel lines often slightly opening as they recede—emphasizing his ever central but ever moving position.

This changing vision, this absence of the restraining blinkers of the single viewpoint, existed in our Western world in classical times. A typical example can be seen in some of the wall paintings, now in the Metropolitan Museum of New York, taken from the room of a house in Boscoreale in southern Italy and dating from the opening of the Christian era. An elaborate urban scene is depicted: buildings of several stories, with projecting balconies and long colonnades, rise one behind the other. There are court-yards, trees, steps, and streets. The spectator grasps the scene from a series of viewpoints, floating about somewhere in front of it, his eye now beneath an overhanging balcony, now above a projecting roof. But each "eyeful," each object upon which his eye momentarily rests, is drawn, as we might say, "correctly."

In a thesis that I have not read, a Greek scholar, Dr. C. A. Doxiades, attempts an explanation of the asymmetric, but certainly carefully planned, disposition of the buildings on the Acropolis at Athens. He represents the field of vision of the eye as an equilateral triangle—with the eye and not the vanishing point as the apex. He then places this human eye at a series of vantage points upon the Acropolis and demonstrates how, from each of these visual stopping places, the eye was presented with a completely organized and balanced architectural scene.

With these examples in mind one can again approach Fatehpur Sikri to see whether they offer us some help in trying to solve the system of thought that underlay its highly intellectual, highly organized and subtle composition that gives the spectator such a sensation of ease and delight.

There are several fairly obvious resting places within the Mahal-i-Khas, the most notable being perhaps the roof of Akbar's private apartments, the terraces of the Panch Mahal (the 5-storied Pleasure Pavilion), the entrance to the Dewan-i-Khas (the Hall of Private Audience) and the balcony overlooking the great outer court, the Dewan-i-Am (Hall of Public Audience). From each of these stations one is presented with a carefully balanced panoramic scene—not with a central objective, it is true, but with a single, coordinated sweep of vision or "eyeful." In each of these cases, the scene has a transparent center and equivalent, but not identical, objects of interest bounding the view to right and left. For instance, from the entrance to the Dewan-i-Khas one glimpses in the center a square pool of water through the transparent columns of an intervening building, flanked to the right by the fantastic hovering terraces of the Panch Mahal and to the left by the curved roof of the state balcony overlooking the Dewan-i-Am. From the terraces of the Panch Mahal, the center is occupied by the space of the Mahal-i-Khas framed by the flamboyant Dewan-i-Khas on the left and the rising structures of Akbar's private apartments on the right.

A panoramic field of vision, moving slowly through some 60 or 90 degrees would seem to be nearer to the visual conception underlying this composition than a single piercing view that demands a central point of interest and undisturbing restful symmetry to either side of it.

It is possible that it is just this panoramic view presented to a moving eye that gives the modern spectator such a feeling of intriguing relaxation at Fatehpur Sikri. But another key to its composition lies quite certainly in the fact that all dimensions, whether of the fashioning of spaces by the disposition of structures or of the spacing of columns, or the size and shape of openings and panels, must have been adjusted to a regulating scale of proportions based certainly upon the square, and probably upon the "golden section." In our Western "academic" schools of architecture of the 19th century the "golden section" was so misused that it became associated with the weakest forms of stylistic architectural mannerisms, but it is significant today that the greatest architect of our time and one of the leaders in the revolt against the dead hand of the academism of the "beaux arts" schools, Le Corbusier, has recently redeveloped a system of measurement of proportions based upon the "golden section" under the name of the "Modulor."

It is now nearly half a century since Western artists and scientists started to break away from the tyranny of the static viewpoint—the conception of a static object and a static universe—to rediscover the importance of vision in motion. This close relationship of the discoveries of artists and scientists is not fortuitous: they are fundamentally one and the same. In Japan, it was not until near the end of the 19th century (after the penetration of Western thought) that there was any word in their language for "Art," meaning "fine art." Until then "Art" had just been "the way of doing" things, whether solving a problem, building a house, or preparing tea. There was "the way," which was difficult and demanded imaginative intelligence and concentration, and there were poor substitutes of "the way." The "artist" as an outcaste of normal society—a mere "Bohemian" or gypsy—is quite a recent Western invention.

Evidences of the fact that our Western vision is changing exist all around us, but most of them are left outside the realm of conscious rationalization, because we have not yet learned to organize them intellectually.

The moving eye is closely with us in the movies and on television. We see the scene from a certain viewpoint, then go nearer—not gradually, but in one swoop—and then look at it again from a totally different angle. We accept this, because this is the way our eye really works: we can, at will, change its focus and alter its position. But we do not connote this at once with the changed appearance of contemporary painting, in which the significant features of these different viewpoints are often presented to us superimposed upon a single sheet, not in a time sequence, but in juxtaposed fragments as, in fact, they are recorded by our mental vision. We have learned to "read" the rapid sequence of viewpoints at the movies, which baffles people who have not had long training in the art of "movie-seeing," but most of us have not given ourselves much practice in learning to read contemporary paintings.

Today we stand before Versailles and are outwardly—and rightly—impressed (but inwardly we find it rather boring). We move along Main Street at night and outwardly—and rightly—confess it is a chaotic mess (but inwardly we find it rather exhilarating). Here is our contemporary urban planning problem: how to find the key to an intellectual system that will help us to organize buildings, color, and movement in space, without relying entirely upon either introspective "intuition" ("I *feel* it to be right that way") or upon the obsolete and static single viewpoint based on the limited optical science of the Renaissance.

PURE COLOR

Fernand Léger

A bare wall is a "dead, anonymous surface." It comes to life only with the help of objects and color. They give it life or destroy it. A stained, colored wall becomes a living element.

Transformation of the wall by color is one of the most thrilling problems of modern architecture. To undertake this mural transformation, color has to be set free. *How?*

Until the pictorial realization by the painters of the last fifty years, color or tone was fast-bound to an object: a dress, body, flower, landscape had the task of wearing color.

To make use of color without reservation, the wall had to be freed to become an experimental field. Color had to be got out, extricated, isolated from the objects in which it had been kept prisoner.

About 1910, with Delaunay, I personally began to liberate pure color in space.

Delaunay developed an experience of his own, keeping the relations of pure complementary colors. I sought a path of my own in an opposite sense, avoiding complementary relations and developing the strength of pure local colors.

In 1912 I got some pure blue and pure red rectangles in the picture *Femme en bleu.*

In 1919, with *La Ville,* pure color, written in a geometrical drawing, was realized at its maximum. It could be static or dynamic; but the most important thing was to have isolated a color so that it had a plastic activity of its own, without being bound to an object.

Modern publicity first understood the importance of this new value: pure tone ran away from paintings, took possession of

roads, and transformed the landscape! New abstract signals—
yellow triangles, blue curves, red rectangles—spread around the
motorist to guide him on his way.

Color was the new object, color set free, color the new reality.

Architects understood its possibilities inside and outside the
building. Wallpaper began to disappear. The white, naked wall
suddenly appeared. One obstacle: its limitations.

The space that I call the "habitable rectangle," is going to be
transformed.

The feeling of a jail—bounded, limited space—is going to
change into boundless colored space.

The habitable rectangle becomes an elastic rectangle. A
light-blue wall draws back, a black wall advances, a yellow wall
disappears. Three selected colors laid out in dynamic contrasts
can destroy the wall. A black piano before a light-yellow wall
creates a visual shock, reducing the habitable rectangle to half
its dimensions.

Our visual education has been symmetrical. Modern scenery
can be absolutely new if we employ asymmetry. From a fixed,
dead condition in which no play, no fancy can be allowed, we're
coming into a new domain that is free.

Living in the Parisian suburbs, I had in my room an old,
large chest on which I put personal objects. I liked to place them
always in an asymmetrical way: the most important object on the
left side, the others in the middle and on the right.

I had a maid, a girl of the people, who cleaned this room
every day. When I came back in the evening, I always found
my objects symmetrically arranged: the most important in the
center and the others symmetrically placed on each side. It was
a silent battle between the maid and me, but a very long fight,
because she thought my objects were placed in a disorderly
fashion.

Perhaps a round house would be the place to study this. It
would be the best place to perceive "the space and visual destruc-
tion of the wall."

The angle has a geometrical resistent strength that is destroyed only with difficulty.

The exterior volume of architecture, its sensitive weight, its distance, can be reduced or increased as a result of the colors adopted.

The "exterior black" can be attacked, in the same way as the interior wall.

Why not undertake the polychrome organization of a street, of a city? During the First World War, I spent my furloughs in Montparnasse; there I met Trotsky, and we often spoke about the thrilling problem of a colored city! He wanted me to go to Moscow because the prospect of a blue street and a yellow street raised enthusiasm in him.

I think that in the urbanism of middle-class housing, the need of a polychrome is most felt. Color set free is indispensable to urban centers.

Polychrome problem, interior and exterior: a shaded view of static façades leading to an attractive centerplace. At this place I conceive of a spectacular, mobile, bright monument with some possibilities of change, giving it the same importance as the church that Catholicism has succeeded so well in imposing upon every village.

Liberated color will play its part in blending new modern materials, and light will be employed to make an orchestration of everything.

An old factory in Rotterdam was dark and sad. The new one was bright and colored: transparent. Then something happened. Without any remark to the personnel, the clothes of the workers became neat and tidy. More neat and tidy. They felt that an important event had just happened around them, within them.

The moral emancipation of a man becoming conscious of three dimensions, of exact volume of weight! This man is no longer a shadow, working mechanically behind a machine. He's a new human being before a transformed daily job. This is tomorrow's problem.

International Paris Exhibition, 1937. The organizers summoned a number of artists to try to find an attractive sensational effect—a spectacular effect that in their minds would bribe the visitors to keep the fête in memory when they went back home. I proposed: Paris all white! I asked for 300,000 unemployed persons to clean and scrape all the façades.

To create a white, bright city! In the evening, the Eiffel Tower, as a conductor of orchestra, with the most powerful projectors in the world, would diffuse along these streets, upon those white, receptive houses, bright, many-colored lights. Airplanes would cooperate in this new fairy scene. Loudspeakers would diffuse melodious music into this new colored world. . . . My project was thrown back.

The cult of the old patinas, of the sentimental ruins; the taste for ramshackle houses, dark and dirty, but so picturesque, are they not? The secular dust that covers the historic, stirring remembrance didn't permit my project the opportunity of realization.

Daily we hear the word "beautiful"; the beautiful bridge, the beautiful automobile. This feeling of beauty, which is awarded to useful constructions, is a proof of the enormous need that men feel within themselves for an escape through art.

The same term is used for a lovely sunset. There is then a common term between natural beauty and manufactured beauty.

Then why not make, why not manufacture the moment of beauty?

Useful for nothing, a magnificent place to repose, which would be a shelter for the anonymous crowd during their enervating day with its hurried rhythm.

It's possible to realize it, with the use of the new liberties, by means of the major arts: color, music, form. Everything set free!

Let us think of former times when so many magnificent temples were built, which mark and express those past civilizations. It's unbelievable that our age should not achieve its popular temples. Architecture, in every period, has been the means of plastic expression most sensitive to the people: the most visual, the most grandiose. It dominates the view, fixes the gaze. Imagine a dazzling point, in which the feeling of bright, light steeples, religions, the need of verticality, high trees, and factory chimneys would be unified, blended.

Man enthusiastically lifts his arms above his head to express his joy in this elevation. To make high and free. Tomorrow's work.

THE PIRATE'S WARDROOM

Stanley Edgar Hyman

In the pirate's wardroom, the dinner service is of solid silver, stamped with the arms of Castile and León. The serving dishes are Sung porcelain. On the walls, paneled in English oak, are a handsome Dutch painting, a pair of crossed dueling pistols that formerly belonged to a French count, a Malay *kris*, and an Inca breastplate in pure soft gold. Everything is of the best, for the pirate captain has natural good taste and an eye for quality. Nothing matches anything else, however, for it has all been stolen piecemeal, in most cases immediately following on the murder of the previous owner.

In my own dining room, where there is neither solid silver nor gold, an Indian miniature from the Rajput Hills jostles an Azande *shongo*, or throwing knife, on the wall, and the shelves are shared uneasily by a group of Australian *churingas*, a terracotta ithyphallic *Silenos* from ancient Thebes, an Iroquois turtle rattle, a collection of Japanese *netsukes*, a Gaboon ship harp, and a Corsican vendetta knife. Although these have all been obtained peaceably, by gift, trade, or purchase, I cannot see that my dining room differs significantly in kind from the pirate's wardroom, or either from André Malraux's "museum without walls," the organizing metaphor of *The Voices of Silence*,[1] which simply raises our small acts of cultural piracy to the level of an aesthetic principle. "In fact our resuscitations are selective," he writes, "and although we have ransacked the ends of the earth, we have not taken over all the arts that came to light." These are the pirate's verbs, and the pirate, too, is selective, more selective in fact than Malraux.

The Voices of Silence is a book about art styles, in their col-

[1] New York, Doubleday & Co., 1953.

lective relations to cultures and their individual relations to artists. It was begun in 1936; some of it appeared in English in *Verve* as early as 1938 (then as now excellently translated by Stuart Gilbert); and a penultimate version was published in three volumes as *The Psychology of Art* from 1947 to 1950. Extensively revised and amplified, these became the four books of the new thick (and presumably final) volume.

The book seems to me to have four principal arguments, somewhat related to one another. The first is the concept of the "museum without walls," the present availability of all the world's arts that we owe to photography. This permits us to see a picture in a context of *all* the artist's work, which gives it "a new significance." This abundance then produces a new selectivity, as we can discover those works uniquely the artist's, in which everything not his characteristic style is stripped away, and reduce our consideration to these, a process Malraux calls making "a true anthology." All modern painting should be treated "anthologically," Malraux says, adding innocently, "more or less." The museum without walls not only gives us this anthology drawn from an artist's entire work but also gives us an art style in its entirety, from which we can similarly make significant selections. Having then anthologized the best work of the best artists, the best examples of the best styles, we can settle happily in our wall-less museum (or wardroom) and appreciate them all. "I do not know of a single great modern painter who does not respond both to certain works by savages and to Poussin," Malraux writes, in a sentence that hardly needs the additional parenthetical reservation, "if in differing degrees."

The book's second argument is a pluralism that starts from Malraux's definition of art as "That whereby forms are transmuted into style." Any forms, so long as some authentic transmutation occurs. "Far from being eclectic and taking pleasure in the diversity of forms, our modern pluralism stems from the discovery of the elements that even the most seemingly disparate works of art have in common," he writes. Invidious aesthetic categories like "retrograde," "barbarian," "primitive," go out the window. Celtic coins are not clumsy imitations of the work of Macedonian *toreutai* but a major style of their own, the work of

Great Masters, and they may be called "barbarian" only in quotes. Similarly, Gothic statues are not botched classical statues, African heads are not unsuccessful realistic portrayals. Prehistoric cave paintings are not merely "a highly developed style"; behind their forms "we surmise other forms."

From this follows a third argument, which we may call "neo-evolutionary," that widely differing cultures have a comparable if not identical development. Malraux writes: "The reason why the life-story of Gandharan art has special interest for the sculptor lies precisely in this fact that, by-passing the intermediate stages of Romanesque and Gothic, it came into line with our Renaissance." One of the book's repeated insistences is that styles are not different ways of "seeing" but aesthetic conventions with histories. Any emphasis on individual expression as a determinant is rejected; Malraux has little use for terms like "instinctive," "inspiration," or "the unconscious." Art styles are born, marry, beget, and die, and the artist's "uniqueness" is only an anecdote in this great biography.

From the sequence of cultural piracy, pluralism, and evolution, Malraux somehow derives a fourth point that is probably the book's principal theme (it gives it its title)—the moral importance of art. "When man faces destiny" through art, "destiny ends and man comes into his own." The arts we value are religious ones, although we do not share their religions; they express "man's ability to escape from chaos, even though the way of escape lies through blood and darkness"; they are "voices of the abyss," of "the dark places of man's heart." The aesthetic impulse is creative, it is "the desire to build up a world apart and self-contained, existing in its own right"; it represents "humanization" in "the deepest, certainly the most enigmatic, sense of the word." "Every masterpiece, implicitly or openly, tells of a human victory over the blind force of destiny"; art speaks "the immemorial language of Man the conqueror"; "All art is a revolt against man's fate."

Malraux argues these theses with a great variety of techniques, shifting imperturbably from close technical criticism of the lines of a Rheims sculpture to the study of the sources of Van Megeeren's Vermeer forgeries, to an illustrated history of

El Greco's development, to a biographical anecdote about Renoir. There must be few types of art scholarship and criticism that do not find a place somewhere in this vast book. His principal device, however, is dichotomy, the creation of opposed poles of imagery, similar to those in G. Wilson Knight's Shakespeare studies. "Provided we have art, not culture, in mind," he writes, "the African mask and Poussin, the ancestor and Michelangelo are seen to be not adversaries, but polarities." On the one hand are "the forms of all that belongs essentially to the human," on the other, "all the forms that crush or baffle man." In the first cluster are "the radiant archetypes": instinct, pleasure, gesture, harmony, the human, uniqueness, specific events, and free will. In the other cluster are "the tragic archetypes": ritual, destiny, hieratic immobility, paralysis, the eternal, nature, attributes, and fatalism.

These polarities are not entirely fixed, in that the ingredients of the second cluster can be transmuted into the first, so that negations become affirmations, by the mysterious powers of art (or Malraux's dialectic). "Our renaissance of the art of savages is more than a rebirth of fatalism," Malraux writes, negating his negation. "I name that man an artist who *creates* forms," he proclaims boldly, but his personal taste seems to be for the creators of the more humanistic forms. At times, particularly in regard to the French moderns, he is extremely all-embracing; at others, like a pictorial Yvor Winters, he reduces Venetian baroque to nine great pictures and names them. The greatest artists for Malraux seem to be Giotto, Rembrandt, and Goya, painters of a markedly humanistic bent, but the seven full-page reproductions that interrupt the text after page 582, and seem to represent Malraux's quintessential anthology, include works by only three European artists, and those three surprising: Vermeer, Piero della Francesca, and Gruenewald.

Even at its most pluralist, Malraux's framework omits a good many art styles and a great deal of art. He argues for a pure plastic art that does not require the social content of Goya or Rembrandt—"the depiction of a world devoid of value can be magnificently justified by an artist who treats *painting itself* as the supreme value"—but these are not the works he seems most to admire. "The paintings of the Pygmies fail to interest us," he writes; "perhaps, indeed, total savagery is incompatible with art." Malraux rejects styles that "pander" to what he calls "delectation" as furiously as did the young Stephen Dedalus of *A Portrait of the Artist as a Young Man,* and he dismisses them similarly as either "sentimental" or "licentious." "No mode of plastic expression is foreign to this universal language," Malraux writes, but surely some are for him, and not only the kinetic arts of delectation. Certain kinds of pictorial stasis do not seem to interest him at all, whether represented by Greek black-figure pottery, Bahuana ivory pendants, or Mondrian.

Malraux persistently treats "ritual and ceremonial symbolism" as a kind of Byzantinism that petrifies the human values of his first cluster, although in practice these elements, whenever he is aware of them, seem to augment a work's meaning and interest for him. Thus he values New Ireland softwood carvings of ancestors, which, he understands, "form the court of the Great Primordial Ancestor, the sculptures in the house of worship suggest him, music is his voice, the festivals converge on him and the dance mimes his gestures as it mimes the tribe's heroic past, the epiphanies of the sun, the moon and death, the fertility of the soil, life-giving rain, the rhythms of the firmament." He has no similar sense of the relationship of myth and ritual to Hopi *kachina* figures; they are only "household gods," and it is significant that a photograph of three of them together is the book's only loveless illustration. On the other hand, in a Celtic coin "the engravers seem harking back, across the chaos of prehistory, to the totemic boar"; Georges de Latour's painting "partakes of the nature of the Mystery-Play, and has the slow rhythms of a rite."

In these cases, both significantly French, myth and rite become "history," and as such Malraux can handle them. History is an important value, but always ambivalent: "The link between history and art often seems so tenuous"; "Though this creative process has a place in history, it is independent of history"; capital-H "History" is in fact our modern equivalent for the Eternal. If the experience of this reader can be taken as typical, a lower-case history is equally involved, the history of experience or familiarity. Thus, of the pictures Malraux reproduces in color, works like El Greco's *View of Toledo* now seem boring, while the exciting works are by unfamiliar painters like Latour and Takanobu, or painters not previously taken seriously (until Malraux pointed out their formal organizations) like Chardin. This capacity to enlarge the reader's horizon is probably the book's greatest value, but its relation to history seems defiantly negative.

The principal opponent Malraux argues against, as W. M. Frohock points out in his able *André Malraux and the Tragic Imagination,* is Oswald Spengler. Frohock shows that *The Voices of Silence* and the latest novel, *Les Noyers de l'Altenburg,* share the same question—"whether it is possible for man to be considered a permanent, continuously identical identity"—and debate it against the same opponent. What the art book calls "the German theory of cultures" is represented in the novel by the anthropologist Moellberg (apparently based on Frobenius). To an American reader, Malraux' argument seems pointed less at Spengler than at a man whose imposition of German philosophy on American thinking we tend to overlook, Franz Boas. We have adopted Hegel's cynical ethical relativism in the form of Boas' cultural pluralism, and Spengler's theory of closed cultures (modified into Wissler's "culture areas") as Boas' restriction of "dynamics" to the record of diffusion and acculturation, rather than polygenesis and evolution. If, as Malraux argues, man is a continuity, culture an evolution, and art an absolute, then Boas must be unwritten and Tylor and Frazer restored, a process we can see already at work in the anthology *Primitive Heritage,* compiled by that reliable bellwether, Margaret Mead.

Another implication of considerable importance in the book is the odd guerrilla warfare conducted against modern abstract painting. There are, Malraux writes, "certain deep-rooted collective emotions, which modern art has chosen to ignore." Something else of value may be substituted—"in a Braque still life the peach no longer has a bloom, the picture has it"—but it is not ultimately adequate. In Malraux's view, a style is coming into being now, "perhaps the greatest style the West has ever sponsored," which "seems to belong to some religion of which it is not aware." It is, he makes clear, a convention of expressive representation, not of abstraction—"a style," not "a calligraphy." "Were our culture to be restricted solely," he writes, "to our response (lively though it is) to forms and colors, and their vivid expression in contemporary art—surely the name of 'culture' could hardly be applied to it." By this time, Malraux has almost completely undermined the book's earlier definition: "Modern art is, rather, the annexation of forms by means of an inner pattern or schema, which may or may not take the shape of objects, but of which, in any case, figures and objects are no more than the expression."

The Voices of Silence is full of genuine insights: that "Rembrandt was the first great master whose sitters sometimes dreaded seeing their portraits," that Dostoevsky has much in common with Byzantine art, that the Middle Ages involve "apotheosis taking the place of incarnation," and many more. It is at the same time a tissue of contradictions: "an art which breaks up into ideograms is regressive" and the "triumph of the sign is a sign of death," but all great art before Christianity had been "a system of signs," the Gandhara carvings make an important rediscovery of "symbolic representation," and all true styles are *"significations."*

The book is full of moving rhetoric: the Buddhist vision sees the world as "two homeless children clasping hands in a dead city, loud with the tedium of apes and the heavy flight of peacocks"; "those monsters of the abyss which the psychoanalyst fishes for with nets, and politics or war, with dynamite"; and its conclusion (at least in English) tolls the authentic Brownian bell: "Survival is not measurable by duration, and death is not assured of its victory, when challenged by a dialogue echoing down the ages." In all this beauty and eloquence, however, there is a good deal of oracular nonsense—"For the artist is by nature secretive and likes to mystify"; "Seldom is a Gothic head more beautiful than when broken"; "The true hero of every fairy story is the fairy"; "Certain African statues, not one curve of whose noses could have been varied by the image-maker without the risk of his being put to death by order of the witch-doctor"—and the discussion of Freud and the Freudian doctrine of wish-fulfillment is shamefully ignorant and foolish.

References to primitive Christianity as "that oriental night-world of blood and doom-fraught stars," to later Christianity as a time when "value was being disintegrated into a plurality of values," to the taste of Augustan Rome as "Second Empire in France," and to Rome in general as soulless, suggest that the author of *The Conquerors* and *Man's Fate* is still at war with a large part of the Western heritage. He nevertheless believes "that, for three hundred years, the world has not produced a single work of art comparable with the supreme works of the West," that "what is challenged in our culture is challenged by the *past* of other cultures," and that the arts of other cultures, their "idols," could not have been appreciated by ours until the present period of enlightenment. We are thus left "sole heir" of the world's bequest and finally are identified as the new Rome—our tastelessness and soullessness tactfully unmentioned—welcoming to our Pantheon "the gods of the defeated."

This Pantheon is, of course, our familiar pirate's wardroom, and here we might pause to note who Malraux speaks for with his omnipresent "we" and "us." Sometimes it is the Western world, sometimes an undefined community of the spirit, sometimes an elite consisting of unnamed modern painters and sculptors, sometimes his readers, and very frequently, I think, only M. Malraux. What *actual* agreement can be presumed? We are all, for example, cultural pluralists (the pirate was a founding father of cultural pluralism), and surely we do not need Malraux to tell us that the time after the fall of Rome was not *really* "dark" nor that Africans (except Pygmies) are not *really* "savages." But how many of us accept the full implications of our belief, and insist that, if Celtic coins and Benin bronzes are comparable to the arts of Greece, then Gaul and Benin had high civilizations comparable to Greece's, and that all previous hierarchies of culture have been foolishly based on literacy alone? And if we believe that certain civilizations are high, then we believe that certain others are low, and we are not cultural pluralists at all. We may even admit to the possession of some ethical absolute from which we can criticize traits in other configurations (would female circumcision in Kenya be an art style, or Buchenwald lampshades?).

If the "primitive" works of art we choose to adopt are not a meaningful part of our own culture, but are not meaningless in our culture either, then most of our previous thinking in this area has been oversimple. Malraux writes, "For us today the mask or the ancestor is no more a magical or a numinous object than a medieval Virgin is *the* Virgin." But neither are our contemporary serious arts magical or numinous, in just this sense. What we need, it seems to me, is a conception of magic as inherent in formal organization, equally present in Picasso's lithographed bulls and the bulls of the Altamira caves, in Klee's *Around the Fish* and in the Australian bark drawing it so much resembles. I think the key to this approach is the word Malraux is so wary of, the word "ritual," and that to attain it he need only extend the way he talks about Latour's painting to cover less representational hieratic organizations.

If we talk of art in terms of symbolic actions that are individual modern equivalents for collective older rites, then a modern poem or picture can once again be discussed as fertility magic, making the metaphoric crops grow in some meaningful sense. This approach sees the work of art, not in narrowly configurational terms, but as functional in a context it carries along with it, out of place and time. In these terms, "culture areas" becomes merely one more outmoded museum category. A thing of beauty is once again that old chestnut, a joy forever, and its origin is irrelevant, because it retains in its formal organization a magical capacity to act on us and initiate us into its rites. At which the pirate chuckles, and goes off to capture a Japanese ship that might be carrying a first-rate Takanobu.

THE ORAL AND WRITTEN TRADITIONS

David Riesman

I want to deal with three large questions: (1) what are the differences between cultures that depend entirely upon the spoken word and those that depend on print; (2) what will be the significance of the written word now that newer mass media have developed; and (3) what is likely to happen in those countries where the tradition of books is not fully established and where newer media are already having a decisive impact.

In the beginning the only word was the spoken word. Anthropologists no longer speak of the peoples they study as primitives, let alone savages; they prefer the less argumentative term "preliterate," and I do not think they are wrong in making literacy the decisive dividing point. There are important differences, of course, between the preliterate tribe that depends entirely on an oral tradition and the peasant culture where illiterate folk dwell within the moral and intellectual ambit of a tradition of written literature, as in China or India. Here we may merely note that, where an oral tradition is exclusive, there is a tendency for the old to have an exalted place as the storage banks of experience and entertainment, whereas writing, as in Egypt, tends to foster hierarchies of skill rather than age.

The impact of the spoken word in a preliterate culture is conveyed in the following passage from a Papago Indian woman's autobiography:

The men from all the villages met at Basket Cap Mountain, and there my father made them speeches, sitting with his arms folded and talking low as all great men do. Then they sang the war songs:

O, bitter wind, keep blowing
That therewith my enemy
Staggering forward
Shall fall.

Many, many songs they sang but I, a woman, cannot tell you all. I know that they made the enemy blind and dizzy with their singing and that they told the gopher to gnaw their arrows. And I know that they called on our dead warriors who have turned into owls and live in Apache country to come and tell them where the enemy were.[1]

From such accounts we become aware of the emotional force that can be harnessed by the spoken or sung word in such a group—so powerful here that it can shatter the morale of a distant enemy and can bring alive the desert with its small creatures slipping like spies through the bush. On such an occasion the quiet voice of the father is resonant with the memories of the tribe. And so, too, on less formal occasions, as when on long winter nights the Papago woman's brothers would say, "My father, tell us something," and her father, lying quietly on his mat, would slowly start to recount how the world began:

Our story about the world is full of songs, and when the neighbors heard my father singing they would open our door and step over the high threshold. Family by family they came, and we made a big fire and kept the door shut against the cold night. When my father finished a sentence we would all say the last word after him.[2]

Implicit here is the fact that a society dependent on oral traditions and oral communications is, by our standards, a slow-paced one: there is time enough, for grownups as well as children, to roll back the carpet of memories.

As long as the spoken or sung word monopolizes the symbolic environment, it is particularly impressive; but once books enter that environment it can never be quite the same again—books are, so to speak, the gunpowder of the mind. Books bring with them detachment and a critical attitude that is not possible in an oral tradition. When a society depends on memory, it employs every device of the demagogue and the poet: rhyme, rhythm, melody, structure, repetition. Since we tend to remember best things most deeply felt, the memorable words in an oral

[1] Ruth Underhill, *Autobiography of a Papago Woman*, Memoir 43, American Anthropological Association, 1936.
[2] *Ibid.*

tradition are often those most charged with group feeling and those which keep alive in the individual the childhood sense of dependence, the terrors and elations of the young and something of their awe for the old. (Indeed, one can hardly speak of *individuals* in the modern sense in such cultures, since individuation depends to some degree on social differentiation and distance.) On the other hand, one thinks of the specialists on recollection in some tribes who can recall the prayers for rain and other ceremonies with word-perfect accuracy: here the individual words have lost affective tone, and rote learning has taken the place of fireside forensics.

Virtually everyone in a preliterate tribe is a specialist in the oral tradition. Eggan reports that in the remote islands of the Philippines messages are conveyed orally with an accuracy fabulous to us, aware as we are that a message or rumor need only pass through two or three persons before becoming unrecognizable. For these tribesmen, words are like buckets in a fire brigade, to be handled with full attention, while we feel we can afford to be careless with the spoken word, backstopped as we are by the written one.

Of course, in another sense we all began life as preliterates; our written tradition is backstopped by an oral one. Adult culture—which is largely the culture of the written word—blots out for most of us our childhood imagery; this gets lost, not, as Freud thought, because it is sexual and forbidden, but because it is irrelevant to us as literate people. We still dream in this earlier, "forgotten language," and our great artists often renew themselves and us by translations from this language into the written vernacular of the adult.

The proverb, as an invented repository of tribal lore and wisdom, is a bridge between the oral and the written stages of history. Edwin Loeb writes that the proverb, as a kind of abstract, generalizing, easily remembered statement about experience—the most literate, so to speak, of the preliterate styles of speech—is associated only with cattle-raising people. It is among such relatively advanced, semi-nomadic people that the need for a distinct body of property laws first tends to be felt—who does

the new calf belong to?—and the proverb is a convenient mne-
monic of tribal judgments. Many of our earliest sacred writings
are collections of proverbs.

The late Harold A. Innis took a rather crabbed, Spenglerian
pleasure in showing that the materials on which words were
written have often counted for more than the words themselves.
For instance, he argues that papyrus, being light and readily
stored in a desert land, put the priests of Egypt in command of
the calendar and, in Big Brother fashion, of social memory and
was essential to the spread of the Egyptian dynasties in space
and the hegemony of the priests in time. The clay tablets of
Sumeria were put out of business by the greater convenience of
the newer forms, just as many downtown movie houses have been
put out of business by TV and the drive-ins. Perhaps it was understandable that a Canadian should be one of the first to study
such problems systematically, after watching his country's forests
being cut down on behalf of the *Reader's Digest* and other forms
of American pulpular imperialism.

The book is one of the first, and very possibly the most important, mass-produced products, and its impact demonstrates
the falsity of the common notion that mass production per se
brings about the massification of men. Print, in replacing the
illuminated manuscript, created the silent, compulsive reader, his
head bobbing back and forth across the lines like a shuttle, working in a monotone of color and a metronome of motion—a semi-
automatic scanner. This, in contrast with the color and variety of
"reading" an illuminated manuscript, where reading was ordinarily aloud, in a group, and where the illustrations enlivened the
occasion, made it more sensuous and less rationalistic. Such reading appears in historical perspective as a transitional stage between the spoken and the silent word, while movies and TV
have brought back some of the qualities and emotional states
associated with the manuscript era.

The book, like the door, is an encouragement to isolation:
the reader wants to be alone, away from the noise of others. This
is true even of comic books for children, who associate comics
with being alone, just as they associate TV with the family, and
movies with friends of their own age.

Thus the book helps liberate the reader from his group and its emotions, and allows the contemplation of alternative responses and the trying on of new emotions. Weber has stressed the importance of the merchant's account book in rationalizing the merchant and his commerce; other historians have made familiar the role of the printed Bible in challenging the authority of the Roman Church. Luther, and especially Calvin, increasing by their doctrine the growing isolation of men, invited each pilgrim to progress by himself, Book in hand, while at the same time trying to institute a new authority in place of the old. But, as the dissident sects of Protestantism illustrate, the book tends to be a solvent of authority: just as there are still blank pages in the merchant's account book waiting to be filled, so there is always the question, when one has challenged traditional authority, "What next?"

At the same time, while the book helped people break away from family and parish, it linked them into noncontiguous associations of true believers. The Polish peasant who learned to read and write became identified with the urban world of progress and enlightenment, of ideology and utopia, even while still in the peasant world. This identification had many of the elements of a conversion, print itself and the world it opened up being a kind of gospel. In this country of near-universal literacy we have forgotten the enthusiasm for print that can burst on people newly literate—the "each one, teach one" movements of Mexico, the Philippines, and elsewhere, the voracity for books (for what most librarians would define as "good" books) in the Soviet Union and other recently industrializing lands. It is no accident that self-taught industrialists like Carnegie became the promoters and patrons of the library movement in America. Among the highly educated, and in countries of long-established literacy, there is little comparable enthusiasm.

Print may be said to mark the epoch of the rise and influence of the middle class—the time-attentive, the future-oriented, the mobile. Reading and education were the highroads this class made use of to rise in the world and to move about in it during the great colonizing periods. Even the novel, denounced as frivolous and sensuous by the Puritans, had an important function in the changing society. I think not so much of its use as a device for reform and civic adult education, as in *Oliver Twist* or *Uncle Tom's Cabin,* as of its less obvious use as a device by which people might prepare themselves for novel contacts and novel life-situations—anticipatory socialization, that is, a preparation in imagination for playing roles that might emerge in one's later career. The very conception of life implicit in the notion of a career is facilitated by the dramatic structure of the novel, especially the *Bildungsroman,* with its protagonist, its interest in motive, its demand on the reader that he project himself into the experiences portrayed. In a society depending on oral tradition, individuals have life-cycles—they live through childhood; they are initiated; they are adult; they grow old; they die—but they do not have careers in our abstract sense of the term. The novel of the 19th century doubtless disoriented many chambermaids and a few duchesses, but on many more occasions it helped prepare individuals for their careers in a disorienting world of rapid industrialization and urbanization—where fictional moves and actual ones were not so unlike, and life and art could almost imitate each other.

If oral communication keeps people together, print is the isolating medium *par excellence.* People who would simply have been deviants in a preliterate tribe, misunderstanding and misunderstood, can through books establish a wider identity—can understand and even undermine the enemies of home and hearth and herd. While the geographic migrations of preliterate peoples have something in common with the incomprehending movements of herds of deer, the readers of the age of discovery were prepared mentally for some of the experiences of their geographic mobility; they had at any rate left home in imagination even if they had not roamed as far or among as strange people as they were actually to meet. The bookish education of these inner-directed men helped harden them for voyages: they wanted to convert the heathen, civilize him, trade with him—if anyone changed in the encounter, it would be the heathen, while they, as they moved about the globe or up the social ladder, remained very much the same men. The epitome of this was the Englishman in the tropics who, all alone, dressed for dinner with home guard ceremonial, toasted the Queen, and, six months late, read with a proper sense of outrage the leader in the London *Times*. His ties with the world of print helped steady him in his course far from home and alone.

Today the successors of these men are often other-directed; they are men molded as much by the mass media outside their education as by their schooling; men who are more public relations-minded than ambitious; men softened for encounters rather than hardened for voyages; if they move about the globe it is often to win the love of the natives or to try to understand their mores, rather than to exploit them for gain or the glory of God. Meanwhile the natives themselves are on the move, and the sharp differences between societies dependent on the oral tradition and those dependent on print are tending to be less important with the coming of radio and film. Often the decisive difference is among the peasants themselves within a country, such as India or the Middle East or Africa—the difference between those who listen to the radio and go to movies and those who shut these things out as the voice of the Devil or as simply irrelevant for them. In the Middle East it was found that those peasants who listened to Radio Ankara or the BBC or the VOA already had, or soon acquired, a different sensibility from those who did not. The former were prepared in the imagination for more voyages than they were likely ever to make. When these peasants were asked what they would do if they were to become President of Turkey, for example, or where they would like to live if they could not live in their native villages, they could answer the questions; they had a stock of opinions—public opinions—on such matters. But the tradition-directed peasants who were not radio listeners or movie-goers could not answer the questions; to the question about becoming President they might say: ". . . How can you ask such a thing? How can I . . . President of Turkey . . . master of the whole world!" The very thought appeared sacrilegious. Nor could such people imagine living anywhere else, and when pressed some said they would die if forced to leave their village.

It is too soon to say whether the epoch of print will be utterly elided in the underdeveloped countries, just as, with the coming of electrical and atomic energy, they may skip the stage of coal and water power. Conceivably, the movies and broadcasting may awaken a hunger for print when their own novelty is worn off and they come to be used as tie-ins with print. Just as the barbarians of Europe in the Middle Ages pulled themselves up by Greek bootstraps, so the nonindustrial countries can for a long time draw on the storehouse of Western science and technology, including the science of social organization; and there are still enough inner-directed men in our society who are willing to go out and help build the armies of Iran and the factories of Istanbul.

READING AND WRITING

H. J. Chaytor

In the medieval world, those who could read or write were the few, and it is likely that most of them did not read or write with our methods or with our facility. In order to gain some idea of the difficulties under which they labored, it is necessary to consider what mental processes are involved in the understanding of spoken or written speech. Psychologists are by no means agreed upon this subject, but most of them would probably accept the following account of its implications.

When we hear the phrase, "Give me that book," the word "book" is recognized as a familiar collocation of sounds; in psychological language, we gain an "acoustic image," which experience enables us to identify. This experience not only includes the recognition of particular sounds but also takes into account pitch, emphasis, and intonation; the individual word "book," spoken in isolation, would evoke an image, but would convey no information stimulating to action, unless such information were provided by gesture or emphasis or intonation. In some languages the isolated word has different meanings, according to the "tone" used by the speaker. All languages are, to some extent, "tone" languages; the simple phrase, "Good morning," may mean, according to the manner of its utterance, "I'm delighted to see you," or, "Here's that infernal bore again"; it may mean, "Thank goodness, he's going," or "Come again when you can."

Experience, therefore, takes into account other matters than the sounds that compose an individual word; but, for the purpose of this analysis, we confine our attention to the word as such. The acoustic image may be translated into the visual image of a book, and, if the hearer is illiterate, this is probably the end of the process. If the hearer can read, he will substitute for the visual image of a book the printed word "book," and in either case there may be a half-felt tendency to articulate the word, a feeling known to psychology as a "kinesthetic" or "speech-motor" image.

When, therefore, a child is learning to read, his task is to construct from printed symbols an acoustic image that he can recognize. When recognition has been achieved, he pronounces the word, not only for the satisfaction of his teacher, but also because he cannot himself understand the printed symbols without transforming them into sounds; he can read only aloud. When he can read faster than he can speak, pronunciation becomes a rapid muttering, and eventually ceases entirely. When this stage has been reached, the child has substituted a visual for an acoustic image, and so long as he continues to be dependent upon printed matter, as most of us are, this condition is never likely to change.

When we read, the visual image of the printed word-form instantaneously becomes an acoustic image; kinesthetic images accompany it, and, if we are not reading aloud, the combination of the two produces "inner speech," which, in the case of most people, includes both inner speaking and inner hearing. It may be that inner pronunciation falls below the threshold of consciousness in the case of those greatly occupied with printed matter; but it will rise to the surface, if the individual begins to read a foreign language in a script with which he is not entirely familiar or to learn by heart a difficult passage that must be orally reproduced verbatim. It is said that some doctors forbid patients with severe throat afflictions to read, because silent reading provokes motions of the vocal organs, though the reader may not be conscious of them. So also when we speak or write, ideas evoke acoustic combined with kinesthetic images, which are at once transformed into visual word images. The speaker or writer can now hardly conceive of language, except in printed or written forms; the reflex actions by which the process of reading or writing is performed have become so "instinctive" and are performed with such facile rapidity that the change from the auditory to the visual is concealed from the reader or writer and makes analysis of it a matter of great difficulty. It may be that acoustic and kinesthetic images are inseparable and that "image" as such is an abstraction made for purposes of analysis, but which is non-existent considered in itself and as pure. But whatever account the individual may render of his own mental processes, and most of us are far from competent in this respect, the fact remains that his idea of language is irrevocably modified by his experience of printed matter.

The result is that we cannot think of language without reference to its written or printed form, and many prefer the printed to the written word, because print is clearer to them; it relieves a strain upon the memory and gives time for deliberate consideration. The hearer to whom a letter has been read will ask to see the script, in order to make sure that he has missed no point; he will take notes of a lecture, lest he should forget matters of interest; no policeman is complete without a pencil to lick and a notebook wherein to scrawl. Visualization can even be an aid to memory; most of us have a clear image, even in advanced age, of certain pages in our first Latin grammar or our first repetition book, and educational writers have begun to realize that the "layout" of the page is almost as important to the learner as the matter that it contains. It is by visual practice that we master the vagaries of English orthography, and so-called bad spellers are often those who are misled by inability to exclude auditory reminiscences; they may be seen, when in doubt, to write down a word on scribbling paper, "to see how it looks," to recover, that is, a visual memory that has become blurred. Hearing and sight, once disconnected, have become inseparable; when we hear a speaker, the effect of his words is transmitted from the auditory to the visualizing capacity, and we see, or can see, the words "in our mind's eye," whether we wish to take notes or not. And when we read to ourselves, the visual impression is accompanied by an auditory perception; we hear, or can hear, the sentences that we read, and when we compose, we write to the dictation of an inner voice.

Sound and sight, speech and print, eye and ear have nothing in common. The human brain has done nothing that compares in complexity with this fusion of ideas involved in linking up the two forms of language. But the result of the fusion is that once it is achieved in our early years, we are for ever after unable to think clearly, independently and surely about any one aspect of the matter. We cannot think of sounds without thinking of letters; we believe letters have sounds. We think that the printed page is a picture of what we say, and that the mysterious thing called "spelling" is sacred. . . . The invention of printing broadcast the printed language and gave to print a degree of authority that it has never lost.[1]

Children can learn languages more easily than adults, because they can concentrate wholly upon audition and are not hampered by habits of visualization; just for that reason, they forget almost as rapidly as they learn, unless they are in continual contact with the language concerned. For the adult to return to the infantile stage of simple auditory perception is a task of extraordinary difficulty for those who are obliged to face it, as, for instance, the missionary who proposes to reduce an unwritten language to writing. He must first learn it as a spoken tongue until he is so fully master of it as to be able to decompose the words he has heard into their component sounds and find a symbol to represent each sound, in fact, to form an alphabet. But in this task, he will be continually hampered by the fact that he has been accustomed to regard language as visualized in the garb of a written orthography.

But when the ordinary well-educated man is learning a new language and hears an unfamiliar word, supposing him to have reached the stage of ability to separate the words of a new language, his instinctive inquiry is how is it spelled? how does it look in writing? from what is it derived, or with what known words is it cognate? Given this help, he can associate the new acquisition with his previous experience and has a chance of making a permanent addition to his vocabulary. But, if he has to depend upon audition alone, he will certainly forget the new word, unless circumstances oblige him to make use of it forthwith and frequently. Such is the consequence of association with print; in printer's ink auditory memory has been drowned and visual memory has been encouraged and strengthened.

Thought, in the full sense of the term, is hardly possible

[1] A. Lloyd James, *Our Spoken Language,* London, Thomas Nelson and Sons, 1938, p. 29.

without words. When ideas arise above the threshold of consciousness, they are formulated by the mind in words; accustomed as we are to import and receive information by means of language, we inevitably follow the same method when we are occupied by mental consideration; we discuss a matter with ourselves as we might discuss it with an interlocutor, and such discussion cannot be conducted without the use of words. Hence, until ideas can be formulated in words, they can hardly be regarded as fully conceived. Here, an objection is raised: unless the thinker possesses words, he cannot think; but, unless he has thought, he cannot possess words; how, then, was the process begun? Did ideas precede language, or is capacity for speech innate and awaiting only the stimulus of ideas provoked by external accident, in order to break into action? In other words, did the hen or the egg come first? This question has interested those concerned with the origins of language, but it does not affect the reality of inner speech as the method of inner thought. This reality has been admitted from the days of Homer to our own time. Odysseus, alone upon his raft and confronted by the rising storm, "in trouble spake to his own great soul" for some twenty hexameter lines; and a public-house orator, describing his domestic troubles, will say, "Then I sez to meself, this 'ere 'as got ter stop," and will conclude his catastrophic narrative, "So I sez to meself, I must 'ave a pint and I comes rahnd 'ere." If the thinker is illiterate, the images that arise in his mind will be auditory; if he is literate, they will be visual; in either case, immediate vocal expression can be given to them, if necessary.

As has been said, this vocal expression is necessary to children who are learning to read or to inexperienced adults; they cannot understand the written or printed symbols without transforming them into audible sounds. Silent reading comes with practice, and when practice has made perfect, we do not realize the extent to which the human eye has adapted itself to meet our requirements. If we take a line of printed matter, cut it lengthwise in half, so that the upper half of the lettering is exactly divided from the lower half, and then hand the slips to two friends, we shall probably find that the man with the upper half will read the line more easily than the man with the lower half.

The eye of the practiced reader does not take the whole of the lettering, but merely so much as will suggest the remainder to his experienced intelligence. Similarly, if we listen to a speaker with a difficult delivery, we instinctively supply syllables and even words that we have failed to hear. Nor does the eye halt at each separate word. When we read our own language, we halt at a point in the line, notice a few letters on either side of it, and proceed to another halting point; the eye has not seen the whole formation of every word, but has seen enough to infer the meaning of the passage. Hence the difficulty of proofreading; our usual method of reading allows us to pass over misprints, because we see enough of any one word to take its correctness for granted. The number of these halting places will vary with the nature of the matter to be read; in a foreign language they will be more numerous than when we are concerned with our own familiar tongue, and if we are reading a manuscript in a crabbed hand with many contractions, we shall be forced to proceed almost letter by letter.

Very different was the case of the medieval reader. Of the few who could read, few were habitual readers; in any case the ordinary man of our own times probably sees more printed and written matter in a week than the medieval scholar saw in a year. Nothing is more alien to medievalism than the modern reader, skimming the headlines of a newspaper and glancing down its columns to glean any point of interest, racing through the pages of some dissertation to discover whether it is worth his more careful consideration, and pausing to gather the argument of a page in a few swift glances. Nor is anything more alien to modernity than the capacious medieval memory, which, untrammeled by the associations of print, could learn a strange language with ease and by the methods of a child, and could retain in memory and reproduce lengthy epic and elaborate lyric poems. Two points, therefore, must be emphasized. The medieval reader, with few exceptions, did not read as we do; he was in the stage of our muttering childhood learner; each word was for him a separate entity and at times a problem, which he whispered to himself when he had found the solution; this fact is a matter of interest to those who edit the writings that he reproduced.[2] Further, as readers were few and hearers numerous, literature in its early days was produced very largely for public recitation; hence, it was rhetorical rather than literary in character, and rules of rhetoric governed its composition.

Even a superficial acquaintance with medieval literature will show that its exponents continued the custom of public recitation common in classical times. The complaint of Juvenal's opening satire may well have been repeated in medieval times. Authors read their works in public, as this was the only way in which they could publish them; Giraldus Cambrensis read his *Topographia Hiberniae* before a public meeting at Oxford for three days in succession to different audiences. Private readings to a circle of friends were more common than these set performances and naturally increased as manuscripts were multiplied and education spread. It was a public perhaps more eager to hear stories than to gather information that supported the numerous professional storytellers, the minstrels and jongleurs who went about the countries and were as necessary to medieval society as was their counterpart in Arab civilization. They performed the business of providing amusement, which has been taken over by the radio and the cinema at the present time.

We gain the majority of our information and ideas from printed matter, whereas the medieval obtained them orally. He was confronted not by the beautiful productions of a university press but by a manuscript often crabbed in script and full of contractions, and his instinctive question, when deciphering a text, was not whether he had seen, but whether he had heard, this or that word before; he brought not a visual but an auditory memory to his task. Such was the result of his upbringing; he had learned to rely on the memory of spoken sounds, not upon the interpretation of written signs. And when he had deciphered a word he pronounced it audibly.[3]

[2] Under the rule of St. Benedict, each monk was to receive a book from the library: "accipiant omnes singulos codices de bibliotheca, quos per ordinem ex integra legant; qui codices in caput Quadragesimae dandi sunt" (Regula, cap. xlviii). No limit of time was set and the books appear to have been returned at the beginning of the succeeding Lent. A year for one book seems a generous allowance; but the slowness of the medieval reader is obvious from this instance.

[3] The process is thus described by a copyist of the 8th century on concluding his work: "Qui scribere nescit nullum putat esse laborem. Tres

If the evidence for this habit of mind and action seems scanty, it must be remembered that early testimony is constantly silent upon subjects concerning which we should like to have information, simply because these matters were so universally common as to pass without comment. As evidence falling within medieval times may be quoted the *Rule of St. Benedict,* chap. xlviii, which ordered the monks "post sextam (horam) surgentes a mensa, pausent in lecta sua cum omni silentio; aut forte qui voluerit legere, sibi sic legat ut alium non inquietet," which suggests that the common manner of reading to oneself meant whispering or muttering. Bernard Pez relates of Richalm of Schönthal: "Oftentimes, when I am reading straight from the book and in thought only, as I am wont, they [devils] make me read aloud by word, that they may deprive me so much the more of the inward understanding thereof, and that I may the less penetrate into the interior force of the reading, the more I pour myself out in exterior speech." This is the case of a man who is trying to accustom himself to silent reading and has not yet formed the habit.

When the eye of a modern copyist leaves the manuscript before him in order to write, he carries in his mind a visual reminiscence of what he has seen. What the medieval scribe carried was an auditory memory and, probably in many cases, a memory of one word at a time.

---

digiti scribunt, duo oculi vident. Una lingua loquitur, totum corpus laborat, et omnis labor, finem habet, et praemium ejus non habet finem" (Wattenbach, *Schriftwesen im Mittelalter,* Leipzig, 1896, p. 495). Three fingers hold the pen, the eyes see the words, the tongue pronounces them as they are written, and the body is cramped with leaning over a desk. The scribe is obviously unable to avoid the necessity of pronouncing each word as he deciphers it.

THE EFFECT OF THE PRINTED BOOK ON LANGUAGE

IN THE 16TH CENTURY

Marshall McLuhan

No sense operates in isolation. Vision is partly structured by ocular and bodily movement; hearing, by visual and kinesthetic experience. Visual space alone would be flat, but acoustic space is always spherical, a nonvisualizable field of simultaneous relations. Yet it's a sphere only in its living dynamics, for it's neither contained in anything nor contains anything. It has no horizons.

Factors making for simultaneous or instantaneous presentations of facts or forces tend to set up fields of relations that have an auditory character. Thus the telegraph supported auditory culture, even though its immediate result appeared as a visual one on the newspaper page. Similarly the photograph tends toward the auditory in giving simultaneously many facts that in writing or speech would take far longer to relate and would have to be recounted, eye-dropper fashion, lineally.

Highly inflectional linguistic structures, spoken or written, have an auditory character; less inflected structures have a visual bias. Complexities of inflection, which for the ear constitute a means of articulation and order, take on a different character when translated phonetically for the eye.

Inflectional complexity, in written form, is not only burdensome for the ear; it's also in conflict with the spatial order that the scanning eye finds natural. To the eye, inflections are not part of the simultaneous order of linguistic variations, which they are for the ear. The reader's eye not only prefers one sound, one tone, in isolation; it prefers one meaning at a time. Simultaneities like puns and ambiguities—the life of spoken discourse—become, in writing, affronts to taste, floutings of efficiency.

Shakespeare's 19th century editors tidied up his text by providing him with grammatical punctuation. They thought to bring out, or hold down, his meaning by introducing a kind of punctuation that came into use more and more after printing. This was an ordering of commas and periods to set off clauses for the eye. But in Shakespeare's time, punctuation was mainly rhetorical and auditory rather than grammatical. The 4th century grammarian Diomedes tells us that punctuation marks indicate an "opportunity for taking breath," and Cassiodorus in his 6th century *Institutio de Arte Grammatica* notes that the *positura or distinctio* is a "suitable pause in a duly measured delivery." For them the function of punctuation for grammatical order was incidental to its function in aiding delivery.

This proportion of stress continued throughout medieval practice, though, in passing on older views of punctuation, medieval writers allowed some recognition of punctuation for grammatical meaning. John of Salisbury in the 12th century noted in his *Metalogicus* that *positurae* mark off the sense, but naturally included the grammatical in the rhetorical as the "sense." Whereas grammar and rhetoric were simultaneous for John of Salisbury, they rapidly became parallel, then remote from each other, as the age of print developed.

Classical-medieval theory and practice persisted through the 16th and 17th centuries. In his *English Grammar* of 1592 Ben Jonson simply observes, like any grammarian, "A comma is a mean breathing, of the sentence going before, and following after. . . ." But print rapidly gave salience to the new visual role of punctuation for which no theoretic justification was forthcoming. To 19th century editors, classical-medieval components of Renaissance punctuation theory were invisible because they were, by then, overlaid by centuries of visual grammatical practice. Phonetic writing reduced the speed of word intake far below the level of oral delivery. Print raised the speed above the level of oral delivery. With phonetic writing came the tendency to read aloud and memorize texts, if only because to re-read them was so excessively tedious compared with the ease of oral repetition from memory. Slowness of manuscript reading necessitated capsulating authors via excerpts, sentences, and summaries. Oral disputation and multi-level comment on texts were the natural result of oral teaching. Multi-level awareness of linguistic phenomena and of audience structure held up during print's first century, but swiftly declined thereafter, since the speedy linear flow of printed language encouraged single perspective in word use and word study.

In More's *Utopia,* 1512, Hythlodaye justifies his refusal to set himself up as a counselor to kings and princes:

> Your scholastic philosophy is not unpleasant among friends in familiar communication, but in the councils of kings, where great matters be debated and reasoned with great authority, these things have no place . . . [for] speculative philosophy thinks all things suitable for all occasions. There is another philosophy that is more urbane, which knows as you would say her own stage, and therefore orders and behaves herself in the play that she has in hand, playing her part accordingly with comeliness, uttering nothing out of due order and fashion.

Clearly, scholastic philosophy was a form of discourse that would not do in the new era. It was doomed, not because of its content or meaning, but because it was chatty, conversational discussion that took all manner of things into account at any given moment. In communication among friends it's natural to interrupt and to interject observations at any point. In such oral interchange there are numerous simultaneous vistas of any topic whatever. The subject is looked at swiftly from many angles: classic notions and insights concerning that subject are, via memory, on the tip of every tongue in the intimate group.

Such an oral form assumes encyclopedism, not specialism. With the coming of print, specialism developed because the individual reader by solitary effort could speed over the superhighways of assembly-line printing without the company or comment of a group of fellow learners and disputants. In his university studies on the 18th century Christopher Wordsworth records how written examinations were introduced at Cambridge when it became impossible for examiners to keep up with the individual reading and studies of their students. As books became cheaper, the quicker and more diligent students discovered that they could acquire knowledge for themselves where previous generations had been dependent on the oral teaching. Then arose the necessity of examination, and, as this has come to be more public, and at last in a sense marketable, there has been a fresh demand for oral instruction.

The passage from *Utopia* indicates More's awareness that specialized matters of state, indeed, the entire traffic of civil and public affairs, call for single perspectives and "due order and fashion." A small amount of traffic permits casual mingling of animals, vehicles, and pedestrians. Heavy traffic calls for strict regulation, whether of vehicles or language. The enormous increase in speed and volume of communication after printing taught the literate public the need for rules and decorum, in grammar, theatre, the arts in general.

Medieval universities were oral in their procedures; they were little hampered by rigidities of administrative apparatus; and they were not grounded by the need for large libraries. Today young lawyers in setting up offices are advised to keep books out of sight: "*You* are the law, the source of all knowledge of the law, so far as your clients are concerned." This was the natural attitude of student to teacher when books were few. It's becoming the attitude again when books are so numerous they are difficult to use or consult.

At Oxford under the Tudors, Mallet tells us, "The old lawless democratic spirit yielded unwillingly to discipline. The Renaissance set up new ideas of learning." The macadamized regularity of administrative procedure, which banished oral variety in prose by 1700, had begun to regulate school and college life much earlier. In place of the lively disputation came the lecture—the single lecturer reading written notes to silent listeners who spent their remaining time in silent reading.

Print enabled one man to speak to many, whereas the readers of any one manuscript were few. Similarly print enabled one reader to read many authors in a few years with the resulting awareness that we now label "historical." One reader speeding through whole eras of the past could return with the illusion of having grasped the unified character of peoples or periods. The manuscript reader went too slowly, traveled too little to develop much time sense. Whatever of the past was discussed was felt as present, just as today the simultaneity and inclusiveness of our historical knowledge makes it all felt as being now. We have arrived once more at the oral via what appear as non-auditory means.

In 16th century dictionaries a word was cited in a series of usable phrases with authors indicated. No attempt was made to isolate meaning in a definition. Before print the very concept of word definition was meaningless, since no single author was read by many people at one period of time. Moreover, it would have been impossible for many people to have consulted any one lexicon. Medievalists say that even nowadays a medieval dictionary would be impossible, since individual writers assumed they were free to define and develop any given term as their thought proceeded.

Print meant the possibility of uniform texts, grammars, and lexicons visually present to as many as asked for them. The classroom, as we know it, was entirely the by-product of print.

It was almost a century after print from movable type began before printers thought to use pagination for readers. Before then pagination was for bookbinders only. With print, the book ceased to be something to be memorized and became a work of reference.

Individual writers throughout the 16th century varied tone sentence by sentence, even phrase by phrase, with all the oral freedom and flexibility of pre-print days. Not until the later 17th century did it become apparent that print called for a stylistic revolution. The speeding eye of the new reader favored not shifting tones but steadily maintained tone, page by page, throughout the volume. It was a change of scenery comparable to that of the motorist who shifts from a road sprinkled with Burma Shave yelps and siren gestures from Miss Rheingold to a throughway or turnpike. By the 18th century the reader could depend on a writer controlling the purr of his sentences and giving him a swift, smooth ride. Prose became urbane, macadamized. The plunging, rearing horses of 16th century journalese were more like a rodeo.

Ingenioso in *The Returne from Parassus* says, "Ile have my

pen run like a spigot and my invention answer it quicke as a drawer," while Nashe gallops breathless and inconsequential in a style calling for the utmost agility of mind and attention:

Verie devout Asses they were, for all they were so dunstically set forth, and such as thought they knew as much of God's minde as richer men: why inspiration was their ordinarie familiar, and buzd in their eares like a Bee in a boxe everie hower what newes from heaven, hell and the land of whipperginnie, displease them who durst, he should have his mittimus to damnation *ex tempore*, they would vaunt there was not a pease difference betwixt them and the Apostles, they were as poor as they, of as base trades as they, and no more inspired than they, and with God there is no respect of persons, onely herein may seem some little diversitie to lurk, that *Peter* wore a sword, and they count it flat hel fire for anie man to weare a dagger: nay, so grounded and gravlled were they in this opinion, that now when they should come to Battell, theres never a one of them would bring a blade (no, not an onion blade) about hym to dye for it.

A popular writer like Shakespeare was free of humanist obsessions about imitation of the ancients. He could exploit the old popular idiom and the huge new tapestry of polyglot effects that poured from the press. Many of his typical effects resulted from pouring the visual masques and pageants of the court and high-life through the new medium of spoken or orated poetry. The learned of the 16th century were obsessed by the need not only to imitate classical poets, but also to adapt this verse to song. Verse had no status at all as recited. It had to be sung. Owing to print, spoken verse became popular on the stage. Song is speech slowed down and adapted to a single tone or pitch. Print made possible the rapid reading of verse. In speeding up song, print fostered oratorically delivered poetry.

While the learned devised laborious reconstructions of Greek theatre in the form of grand opera, Shakespeare played with the new fabric and colors of the vernacular as enriched by a flood of translation from Latin, Spanish, French, Italian. When Donne and the Metaphysicals took over this new spoken verse for lyric poetry, they took over its heavy visual emphasis. So conscious were they of this visual stress, they reverted to the pictorial lore of the primitive *Biblia Pauprum*.

Between the 13th and 16th centuries word order substituted for word inflection as a principle of grammatical syntax. The same tendency occurred with word formation. After printing both tendencies accelerated greatly, and there was a shift from audible to visual means of syntax. Charles Fries writes:

In Old English this relationship of modification (the character-substance or modifier-noun relationship) was indicated primarily by means of inflectional forms. Thus in such a sentence as *on aenium otherum mystres thingum* it is quite clear that *otherum* must go with *thingum*, for the case form of both words is dative plural. We are compelled to say "in any other things of the monastery" for plural. In Modern English *other* can be made to modify *things* only by being placed immediately before it. . . . It was not until the Middle English period that the collective noun singular in form appeared with any frequency *immediately* followed or preceded by a plural verb form. Collective nouns ever since, however, had in English a concord of number which depended on the meaning emphasized rather than on the form of the noun. In other words, the pattern concerning the use of number forms in secondary words that has emerged in the development of English is a concord based primarily on the number idea emphasized in the primary word rather than on its form.[1]

Edward P. Morris, writing *On Principles and Methods in Latin Syntax,* says:

The general movement by which single words have in part taken the place of inflection is the most sweeping and radical change in the history of the Indo-European languages. It is at once the indication and the result of a clearer feeling of concept-relation. *Inflection in the main rather suggests than expresses relations;* it is certainly not correct to say that in every case the expression of relation by a single word, e.g., a preposition, is clearer than the suggestion of the same relation by a case form, but it is correct to say that the relation can become associated with a single word only when it is felt with a considerable degree of clearness. The relation between concepts must itself become a concept. To this extent *the movement toward the expression of relation by single words is a movement toward precision.* . . . The adverb-preposition is the expression in more distinct form of some element of meaning which was latent in the case-form. It serves therefore as a definition of the meaning of the case-form.[2]

[1] *American English Grammar,* New York, Appleton-Century-Crofts, Inc., 1940, pp. 256, 49.
[2] New York, Charles Scribner's Sons, 1902, pp. 102, 103-4.

Now behind us are those unimaginative centuries that strove to eliminate ambiguity and suggestion from language in the interests of "the one clear meaning." Recovery of auditory imagination with its awareness of the total life of words has banished the tyranny of visual, printed forms of language with their intolerance of complex modes.

The inflectional suggests, rather than expresses or spells out, relations. Technology is explicitness. Writing was a huge technological advance in this respect. It expressed, it made explicit, many relations that were implicit, suggested in inflectional language structures. And what writing couldn't make explicit quickly got lost. Far more than writing, printing was a technological means of explicitness and explication. But those auditory inflections and relations which could not be made visually explicit by print were soon lost to the language—except for dialects and Vulgar English, of course.

As a result of these changes there remain in English only six forms (me, us, him, them, her, whom) to distinguish the dative or the accusative from the nominative, and the six case forms of these pronouns in their modern use do not function in the conveying of grammatical ideas. These are the words that create most of the booby traps of English for the semiliterate. The whole problem is to manage their auditory patterns in relation to a half-learned visual or word-position grammar. As with punctuation straddling between a rhetorical and a syntactical function, so with these relics of auditory and inflectional English. Their users are unaware that the trick is to ignore the visual relations of words when handling these mavericks. This confusion is true of the other grammatical forms as well. Fries writes:

The growing importance of word order as a grammatical device to show the relation between substantive and verb since the early 15th century has had an important effect upon the use of these six dative-accusative forms. Certain positions in the English sentence have come to be felt as "subject" territory, others as "object" territory and the forms of the words in each territory are pressed to adjust themselves to the character of that territory. The dative-accusative forms, with no real function of their own but used only as an accompaniment of other devices offer very little resistance to the pressures of word order.

Our Modern English "I was given a book" furnished a good illustration of the pressure of word order. The Old English "Me waes gegiefen an boc," with the dative pronoun standing first, was a common construction. It is only after word order had become a vigorous device for the showing of grammatical relationships that the dative *me* standing in "subject" territory was changed to the nominative I. Ever since the 16th century this new construction has been normal English practice in spite of the protests of certain grammarians. The dative with impersonal verbs which appeared frequently in Old and Middle English also shows the pressure of word order as these constructions were replaced by the nominative form of the pronoun and the personal verb. *Him likode* became *He liked*. *Me greues* became *I grieve*. Altogether it is only in the few places where the pressures of word order conflict with the inertia of an older practice that problems arise concerning the use of these case forms of pronouns. In nearly all situations the older practice concerning the inflections (similar to that of Latin) agrees with the newer pressures of word order. . . .

In the matter of person, the distinct verb forms have tended to disappear and no new device has taken their place; in the matter of mood, however, the passing of the inflections has been accompanied by a greatly increased use of the so-called modal auxiliaries—the function words used to express an emotional attitude toward the action or state. In Old English there were distinctive verb forms for the subjunctive in both the present tense and the preterit. Within the subjunctive singular and plural number forms were clearly separated, but there were no forms to distinguish person. These distinctive subjunctive forms, in the course of our language development, fell together with those of the indicative mode, until, in Present-day English, but one form remains, in all verbs except the verb *to be*, to separate subjunctive mood from indicative. In Present-day English, as in the past, the subjunctive has no distinct forms for the various persons, whereas the indicative still retains the -*s* of the third person singular. As a matter of fact, however, this *s*-less subjunctive very rarely appears, and then in Vulgar English: "So *help* me God," "God *bless* you and *speed* you on," "*insisted* that he join the army." [3]

Only the indicative remains and what could be more striking about its one-level lineality than the fact we have altered the

[3] Charles Fries, *op. cit.*, pp. 90, 103.

meaning of the word from *dico* to pointing or indicating in a non-auditory mode. Once the dynamics of language begin to shift to the visual mode, past, present, and future become the only time senses that make sense, because they are the only ones that can be indicated to the reader of a page. All those subtle time and mood relations natural to preliterate language and to the simultaneous order of the auditory language are swiftly sheared away by the assembly lines of the typesetter.

The explicit technology of written and especially printed codifications of language inherently favors any tendency to develop or utilize monosyllables as a source of new word formation. Everything we know about technology points to its natural bent for the replaceable part and the snug unit that can serve many roles.

The disappearance of the final -*e*, still retained by most verb forms till the 15th century, released many words to function both as noun and verb. This development gave great flexibility to 16th century usage, but was not peculiar to that period, having continued unabated. In fact, the newspaper headline jungle is probably richer today in words with dual noun-verb functions than the Elizabethan period. Monosyllabism has been given more development by newspaper headlines than by all other factors combined. With headlines, the purely visual aspect of print accelerated rather than originated. But the headline only gives acute stress to factors inherent in phonetic writing, emergent in print, and obvious in the newspaper:

EPSOM SALTS WONT WORK

STIX NIX HIX PIX

BERRAS BIG BAT BANISHES BUMS

LONDON FIDDLES WHILE BURNS ROAMS

UNDERCOVER MEN UNCOVER UNDERWEAR

UNDERWORLD

While the power press, fed by the telegraph, frantically promoted monosyllabism and action verb headlines, literary men were justifying this development by theories about the superiority of simple colloquial Anglo-Saxon English. Jespersen writes of the phenomenon of back-formation, which occurs entirely as a result of word appearance: "The adverbs *sideling, groveling* and *darkling* were originally formed by means of the adverbial ending -*ling*, but in such phrases as 'he walks sideling,' 'he lies groveling,' etc., they looked exactly like participles in -*ing*, and the consequence was that the new verbs to sidle, to grovel, and to darkle were derived from them by the subtraction of -*ing*." But why should it be only in some trivial backwater of back-formation that the Jespersens notice the power of visuality in linguistic change?

Printed grammars since the 18th century created a fog based on the concept of correctness. Once this concept, unconsciously derived from the form of print itself, was pervasive, any hope of study of the actual dynamics of our language situation was obliterated. Our new media with their complex influence on language are similarly blanketed today.

LINEAL AND NONLINEAL CODIFICATIONS OF REALITY

Dorothy Lee

The following study is concerned with the codification of reality and, more particularly, with the nonlineal apprehension of reality among the people of the Trobriand Islands, in contrast to our own lineal phrasing. Basic to my investigation is the assumption that a member of a given society—who, of course, codifies experienced reality through the use of the specific language and other patterned behavior characteristic of his culture —can actually grasp reality only as it is presented to him in this code. The assumption is not that reality itself is relative but that it is differently punctuated and categorized, by participants of different cultures, or that different aspects of it are noticed by, or presented to, them. If reality itself were not absolute, then true communication of course would be impossible. My own position is that there is an absolute reality and that communication is possible. If, then, that which the different codes refer to is ultimately the same, a careful study and analysis of a different code, and of the culture to which it belongs, should lead us to concepts that are ultimately comprehensible, when translated into our own code. It may even, eventually, lead us to aspects of reality from which our own code excludes us.

It is a corollary of this assumption that the specific phrasing of reality can be discovered through intensive and detailed analysis of any aspect of culture. My own study was begun with an analysis of linguistic formulation, only because it is in language that I happen to be best able to discover my clues. To show how these clues can be discovered and used as guides to the apprehension of reality, as well as to show what I mean by codification, I shall present at first concrete material in the field of language.

Diversity of Codification

That a word is not the reality, not the thing that it represents, has long been a commonplace to all of us. The thing that I hold in my hand as I write *is* not a pencil; I *call* it a pencil. And it remains the same whether I call it *pencil, molyvi, Bleistift,* or *siwiqoq.* These words are different sound-complexes applied to the same reality; but is the difference merely one of sound-complex? Do they refer to the same *perceived* reality? *Pencil* originally meant little tail; it delimited and named the reality according to form. *Molyvi* means lead and refers to the writing element. *Bleistift* refers both to the form and to the writing-element. *Siwiqoq* means painting-stick and refers to observed function and form. Each culture has phrased the reality differently. To say that *pencil,* for example, applies primarily to form is no idle etymological statement. When we use this word metaphorically, we refer neither to writing element nor to function, but to form alone; we speak of a pencil of light, or a styptic pencil.

When I used the four words for this object, we all knew what reality was referred to; we knew the méaning of the word. We could visualize the object in my hand, and the words all delimited it in the same way; for example, none of them implied that it was a continuation of my fist. But the student of ethnography often has to deal with words that punctuate reality into different phrasings from the ones with which he is familiar. Let us take, for instance, the words for "brother" and "sister." We go to the islands of Ontong Java to study the kinship system. We ask our informant what he calls his sister and he says *ave;* he calls his brother *kainga.* So we equate *ave* with "sister" and *kainga* with "brother." By way of checking our information we ask the sister what she calls her brother; it turns out that for her, *ave* is "brother," not "sister," as we were led to expect, and that it is her sister whom she calls *kainga.* The same reality, the same actual kinship is present there as with us; but we have chosen a different aspect for naming. We are prepared to account for this; we say that both cultures name according to what we would call a certain type of blood-relationship; but, whereas we make reference to absolute sex, they refer to relative sex. Further inquiry, however, discloses that in this, also, we are wrong. Because in our own culture we name relatives according to formal definition and biologic relationship, we have thought that this formulation represents reality; and we have tried to understand the Ontong Javanese relationship terms according to these distinctions, which, we believe, are given in nature. But the Ontong Javanese classifies relatives according to a different aspect of reality, differently punctuated. And because of this, he applies *kainga* as well to a wife's sister and a husband's brother; to a man's brother's wife and a woman's sister's husband as well as to a number of other individuals. Neither sex nor blood-relationship, then, can be basic to this term.

The Ontong Javanese name according to their everyday behavior and experience, not according to formal definition. A man shares the ordinary details of his living with his brothers and their wives for a large part of the year; he sleeps in the same large room, he eats with them, he jokes and works around the house with them; the rest of the year he spends with his wife's sisters and their husbands, in the same easy companionship. All these individuals are *kainga* to one another. The *ave*, on the other hand, names a behavior of great strain and propriety; it is based originally upon the relative sex of siblings, yes, but it does not signify biologic fact. It names a social relationship, a behavior, an emotional tone. *Ave* can never spend their adult life together, except on rare and temporary occasions. They can never be under the same roof alone together, cannot chat at ease together, cannot refer even distantly to sex in the presence of each other, not even to one's sweetheart or spouse; more than that, everyone else must be circumspect when the *ave* of some-one of the group is present. The *ave* relationship also carries special obligations toward a female *ave* and her children. *Kainga* means a relationship of ease, full of shared living, or informality, gaiety; *ave* means one of formality, prohibition, strain.

These two cultures, theirs and our own, have phrased and formulated social reality in completely different ways and have given their formulation different names. The word is merely the name of this specific cultural phrasing. From this one instance we might formulate the hypothesis—a very tentative one—that among the Ontong Javanese names describe emotive experiences, not observed forms or functions. But we cannot accept this as fact, unless further investigation shows it to be implicit in the rest of their patterned behavior, in their vocabulary and the morphology of their language, in their ritual and their other organized activity.

One more instance, this time from the language of the Wintu Indians of California, will deal with the varying aspect or segmentation of experience that is used as a basis of classification. To begin with, we take the stem *muk*. On the basis of this stem we form the word *mukeda*, which means "I turned the basket bottom up"; we form *mukuhara*, which means "The turtle is moving along"; and we form *mukurumas*, which means "automobile." Upon what conceivable principle can an automobile be put in the same category as a turtle and a basket? There is such a principle, however, and it operates also when the Wintu calls the activity of laundering *to make foam continuously*. According to this principle, he uses the same stem (*puq* or *poq*) to form words for the following:

> *puqeda:* I just pushed a peg into the ground.
> *olpuqal:* He is sitting on one haunch.
> *poqorahara:* Birds are hopping along.
> *olpokoyabe:* There are mushrooms growing.
> *tunpoqoypoqoya:* You walked short-skirted, stiff-legged ahead of me.

It is difficult for us to discover the common denominator in the different formations from this one stem, or even to believe that there can be one. Yet, when we discover the principle underlying the classification, the categories themselves are understandable. Basic to the classification is the Wintu view of himself as observer; he classifies as an outsider. He passes no judgment on essence, and, where we would have used kinesthetic or participatory experience as the basis of naming, he names as an observer only, for the shape of the activity or the object. The turtle and the automobile can thus naturally be grouped together with the inverted baskets. The mushroom standing on its stem, the fist grasping a peg against the ground, the stiff leg topped by a short skirt, or by the body of a bird or of a man resting on a haunch, obviously all belong together in one category. But the progress of a grasshopper cannot be categorized with that of a hopping bird. We, who classify on a different basis, apprehend the hop of the two kinesthetically and see it as basically the same in both cases; but the Wintu see the difference in recurrent shape, which is all-important to them, and so name the two by means of completely different stems. Again, when we discover this principle, it is easy to see that from the observer's point of view laundering is the making of a lot of foam and to see why, when beer was introduced, it was named *laundry*.

An exhaustive study of the language and other aspects of Wintu culture shows that this principle is present in all of the Wintu language, as well as in the Wintu's conception of the self, of his place in the universe, in his mythology, and probably in other aspects of his culture.

Nonlineality in Trobriand Language

I have discussed at length the diversity of codification of reality in general, because it is the foundation of the specific study that I am about to present. I shall speak of the fomulation of experienced reality among the Trobriand Islanders in comparison with our own; I shall speak of the nature of expectancy, of motivation, of satisfaction as based upon a reality that is differently apprehended and experienced in two different societies; which is, in fact, for each, a different reality. The Trobriand Islanders were studied by the late Bronislaw Malinowski, who has given us the rich and circumstantial material about them that has made this study possible. I have given a detailed presentation of some implications of their language elsewhere; but since it was in their language that I first noticed the absence of lineality, which led me to this study, I shall give here a summary of the implications of the language.

A Trobriand word refers to a self-contained concept. What we consider an attribute or a predicate is to the Trobriander an ingredient. Where I would say, for example, "a good gardener," or "the gardener is good," the Trobriand word would include both "gardener" and "goodness"; if the gardener loses the goodness, he has lost a defining ingredient, he is something else, and he is named by means of a completely different word. A *taytu* (a species of yam) contains a certain degree of ripeness, bigness, roundedness, etc.; without one of these defining ingredients, it is something else, perhaps a *bwanawa* or a *yowana*. There are no adjectives in the language; the rare words dealing with qualities are substantivized. The term *to be* does not occur; it is used neither attributively nor existentially, since existence itself is contained; it is an ingredient of being.

Events and objects are self-contained points in another respect; there is a series of beings, but no becoming. There is no temporal connection between objects. The taytu always remains itself; it does not *become* overripe; overripeness is an ingredient of another, a different, being. At some point, the taytu *turns into* a yowana, which contains overripeness. And the yowana, overripe as it is, does not put forth shoots, does not *become* a sprouting yowana. When sprouts appear, it ceases to be itself; in its place appears a *silasata*. Neither is there a temporal connection made—or, according to our own premises, perceived—between events; in fact, temporality is meaningless. There are no tenses, no linguistic distinction between past or present. There is no arrangement of activities or events into means and ends, no casual or teleologic relationships. What we consider a casual relationship in a sequence of connected events is to the Trobriander an ingredient of a patterned whole. He names this ingredient *u'ula*. A tree has a trunk, u'ula; a house has u'ula, posts; a magical formula has u'ula, the first strophe; an expedition has u'ula, a manager or leader; and a quarrel contains an u'ula, what we would call a cause. There is no purposive *so as to;* no *for the purpose of;* there are no *why* and no *because*. The rarely used *pela,* which Malinowski equates with *for,* means primarily *to jump*. In the culture, any deliberately purposive behavior—the kind of behavior to which we accord high status—is despised. There is no automatic relating of any kind in the language. Except for the rarely used verbal it-differents and it-sames, there are no terms of comparison whatever. And we find in an analysis of behavior that the standard for behavior and of evaluation is non-comparative.

These implications of the linguistic material suggest to my mind an absence of axiomatic lineal connection between events or objects in the Trobriand apprehension of reality, and this implication, as I shall attempt to show below, is reinforced in their definition of activity. In our own culture, the line is so basic that we take it for granted, as given in reality. We see it in visible nature, between material points, and we see it between metaphorical points such as days or acts. It underlies not only our thinking but also our aesthetic apprehension of the given; it is basic to the emotional climax, which has so much value for us, and, in fact, to the meaning of life itself. In our thinking about personality and character, we have assumed the line as axiomatic.

In our academic work, we are constantly acting in terms of an implied line. When we speak of *ap*plying an *at*tribute, for example, we visualize the process as lineal, coming from the outside. If I make a picture of an apple on the board, and want to show that one side is green and the other red, I connect these attributes with the pictured apple by means of lines, as a matter of course; how else would I do it? When I organize my data, I *draw* conclusions *from* them. I *trace* a relationship between my facts. I describe a pattern as a *web* of relationships. Look at a lecturer who makes use of gestures; he is constantly making lineal connections in the air. And a teacher with chalk in hand will be drawing lines on the board whether he be a psychologist, a historian, or a paleontologist.

Preoccupation with social facts merely as self-contained facts is mere antiquarianism. In my field, a student of this sort would be an amateur or a dilettante, not an anthropologist. To be an anthropologist, he can arrange his facts in an upward slanting line, in a *unilinear* or *multilinear course* of development, in *parallel lines* or *converging lines*. Or he may arrange them geographically, with *lines of diffusion* connecting them; or schematically, using *concentric circles*. Or, at least, he must indicate what his study *leads to*, what new insights we can *draw from* it. To be accorded status, he must use the guiding line as basic.

The line is found or presupposed in most of our scientific work. It is present in the *induction* and the *deduction* of science and logic. It is present in the philosopher's phrasing of means and ends as lineally connected. Our statistical facts are presented lineally as a *graph* or reduced to a normal *curve*. And all of us, I think, would be lost without our diagrams. We *trace* a historical development; we *follow the course* of history and evolution *down to* the present and *up from* the ape; and it is interesting to note, in passing, that, whereas both evolution and history are lineal, the first goes up the blackboard, the second goes down. Our psychologists picture motivation as external, connected with the act through a line, or, more recently, entering the organism through a lineal channel and emerging transformed, again lineally, as response. I have seen lineal pictures of nervous impulses and heartbeats, and with them I have seen pictured lineally a second of time. These were photographs, you will say, of existing fact, of reality—a proof that the line is present in reality. But I am not convinced, perhaps due to my ignorance of mechanics, that we have not created our recording instruments in such a way that they have to picture time motion, light and sound, heartbeats and nerve impulses lineally, or that the unquestioned assumption of the line is axiomatic. The line is omnipresent and inescapable, and so we are incapable of questioning the reality of its presence.

When we see a *line* of trees, or a *circle* of stones, we assume the presence of a connecting line that is not actually visible. And we assume it metaphorically when we follow a *line* of thought, a *course* of action, or the *direction* of an argument; when we *bridge* a gap in the conversation, or speak of the *span* of life or of teaching a *course*, or lament our *interrupted career*. We make children's embroidery cards and puzzle cards on this assumption; our performance tests and even our tests for sanity often assume that the line is present in nature and, at most, to be discovered or given visual existence.

But is the line present in reality? Malinowski, writing for members of our culture and using idiom that would be comprehensible to them, describes the Trobriand village as follows: "Concentrically with the circular row of yam houses there runs a ring of dwelling huts." He saw, or, at any rate, he represented, the village as two circles. But in the texts he recorded, we find that the Trobrianders at no time mention circles or rings or even rows when they refer to their villages. Any word they use to refer to a village, such as *a* or *this*, is prefixed by the substantival element *kway*, which means *bump* or *aggregate of bumps*. This is the element they use when they refer to a pimple or a bulky rash, or to canoes loaded with yams. In their terms, a village is an aggregate of bumps; are they blind to the circles? Or did Malinowski create the circles himself, out of his cultural axiom?

Again, for us as well as in Malinowski's description of the Trobrianders, which was written necessarily in terms meaningful to us, all effective activity is certainly not a haphazard aggregate of acts, but a lineally planned series of acts leading to an envisioned end. Their gardening with all its specialized activities, both technical and magical, leading to a rich harvest; their *kula* involving the cutting down of trees, the communal dragging of the tree to the beach, the rebuilding or building of large seaworthy canoes, the provisioning, the magical and ceremonial activities involved—surely all these can be carried through only if they are lineally conceived. But the Trobrianders do not describe their activity lineally; they do no dynamic relating of acts; they do not use even so innocuous a connective as *and*. Here is part of a description of the planting of coconut: "Thou-approach-there coconut thou-bring-here-we-plant-coconut thou-go thou-plant our coconut. This-here it-emerge sprout. We-push-away this we-push-away this-other coconut-husk-fiber together sprout it-sit together root." We, who are accustomed to seek lineal continuity, cannot help supplying it as we read this; but the continuity is not given in the Trobriand text; and all Trobriand speech, according to Malinowski, is "jerky," given in points, not in connecting lines. The only connective I know of in Trobriand is the *pela*, which I mentioned above, a kind of preposition that also means "to jump."

I am not maintaining here that the Trobrianders cannot see continuity; rather, that lineal connection is not automatically made by them, as a matter of course. At Malinowski's persistent questioning, for example, they did attempt to explain their activities in terms of cause or motivation, by stating possible "results" of uncooperative action. But Malinowski found their answers confused, self-contradictory, inconsistent; their preferred answer was, "It was ordained of old"—pointing to an ingredient value of the act instead of giving an explanation based on lineal connection. And when they were not trying to find answers to leading questions, the Trobrianders made no such connections in their speech. They assumed, for example, that the validity of a magical spell lay not in its results, not in proof, but in its very being: in the appropriateness of its inheritance, in its place within the patterned activity, in its being performed by the appropriate person, in its realization of its mythical basis. To seek validity through proof was foreign to their thinking, yet they attempted to do so at the ethnographer's request. I should add here that their names for constellations imply that here they see lineal figures; I cannot investigate the significance of this, as I have no contextual material. At any rate, I would like to emphasize that, even if the Trobriander does occasionally supply connecting lines between points, his perception and experience do not automatically fall into a lineal framework.

The fact remains that Trobrianders embark on, what is certainly for us, a series of acts that "must require" planning and purposiveness. They engage in acts of gift-giving and gift-receiving that we can certainly see as an exchange of gifts. When we plot their journeys, we find that they do go from point to point, they do navigate a course, whether they say so or not. Do they merely refrain from giving linguistic expression to something they actually recognize in nature? On the non-linguistic level, do they act on an assumption of a lineality that is given no place in their linguistic formulation? I believe that, where valued activity is concerned, the Trobrianders do not act on an assumption of lineality at any level. There is organization or rather coherence in their acts because Trobriand activity is patterned activity. One act within this pattern gives rise to a preordained cluster of acts. Perhaps one might find a parallel in our culture in the making of a sweater. When I embark on knitting one, the ribbing at the bottom does not *cause* the making of the neckline, nor of the sleeves or the armholes; and it is not a part of a lineal series of acts. Rather, it is an indispensable part of a patterned activity that includes all these other acts. Again, when I choose a dress pattern, the acts involved in the making of the dress are already present for me. They are embedded in the pattern I have chosen. In this same way, I believe, can be seen the Trobriand insistence that though intercourse is a necessary preliminary to conception, it is not the cause of conception. There are a number of acts in the pattern of procreating; one is intercourse; another, the entrance of the spirit of a dead Trobriander into the womb. However, there is a further point here. The Trobrianders, when pressed by the ethnographer or teased by the neighboring Dobuans, showed signs of intense embarrassment, giving the impression that they were trying to maintain unquestionably a stand in which they had to believe. This, I think, is because pattern is truth and value for them; in fact, acts and being derive value from the embedding pattern.

So the question of perception of line remains. It is because they find value in pattern that the Trobrianders act according to nonlineal pattern, not because they do not perceive lineality.

But all Trobriand activity does not contain value; and when it does not, it assumes lineality, and is utterly despicable. For example, the pattern of sexual intercouse includes the giving of a gift from the boy to the girl; but if a boy gives a gift so as to win the girl's favor, he is despised. Again, the kula pattern includes the eventual reception of a gift from the original recipient; the pattern is such that it keeps the acts physically and temporally completely disparate. In spite of this, however, some men are accused of giving gifts as an inducement to their kula partner to give them a specially good kula gift. Such men are labeled with the vile phrase: he barters. But this means that, unvalued and despised, lineal behavior does exist. In fact, there are villages in the interior whose inhabitants live mainly by bartering manufactured articles for yams. The inhabitants of Omarakana, about whom Malinowski's work and this study are mainly concerned, will barter with them, but consider them pariahs.

This to say that it is probable that the Trobrianders experience reality in nonlineal pattern because this is the valued reality and that they are capable of experiencing lineally, when value is absent or destroyed. It is not to say, however, that this, in itself, means that lineality is given, is present in nature, and that pattern is not. Our own insistence on the line, such as lineal causality, for example, is often based on unquestioned belief or value. To return to the subject of procreation, the husband in our culture, who has long hoped and tried in vain to beget children, will nevertheless maintain that intercourse causes conception, perhaps with the same stubbornness and embarrassment the Trobrianders exhibited when maintaining the opposite.

Absence of Line as Guide

The line in our culture not only connects but also moves. And as we think of a line moving from point to point, connecting one to the other, so we conceive of roads as *running from* locality *to* locality. A Trobriander does not speak of roads either as connecting two points or as *running from* point *to* point. His paths are self-contained, named as independent units; they are not *to* and *from*, they are *at*. And he himself is *at*; he has no equivalent for our *to* or *from*. There is, for instance, the myth of Tudava, who goes—in our view—from village to village and from island to island planting and offering yams. The Trobriand text puts it this way: "Kitava it-shine village already [i.e., completed] he-is-over. 'I-sail I-go Iwa; Iwa he-anchor he-go ashore. . . . He-sail Digumenu. . . . They-drive [him off] . . . he-go Kwaywata." Point after point is enumerated, but his sailing from and to is given as discrete event. In our view, he is actually following a southeasterly course, more or less; but this is not given as course or line, and no directions are even mentioned. In fact, in the several texts referring to journeyings in the Archipelago, no words occur for the cardinal directions. In sailing, the "following" winds are named according to where they are *at*, the place where they strike the canoe, such as wind-striking-the-outrigger-beam, not according to where they *come from*. Otherwise, we find names for the southwest wind (youyo), and the northwest wind (bombatu), but these are merely substantival names that have nothing to do with direction, names for kinds of wind.

When a member of our society gives an unemotional description of a person, he follows an imaginary line, usually downward: from head to foot, from tip to toe, from hair to chin. The Navaho do the opposite, following a line upward. The Trobriander follows no line, at least none that I can see. "My head boils," says a kula spell; and it goes on to enumerate the parts of the head as follows: nose, occiput, tongue, larynx, speech, mouth. Another spell, casting a protective fog, runs as follows: "I befog the hand, I befog the foot, I befog the head, I befog the shoulders. . . ." There is a magic formula where we do recognize a line, but it is one Malinowski did not record verbatim at the time; he put it down later from memory, and it is not improbable that his memory edited the formula according to the lineality of his culture. When the Trobriander enumerates the parts of a canoe, he does not follow any recognizable lineal order: "Mist . . . surround me my mast . . . the nose of my canoe . . . my sail . . . my steering oar . . . my canoe-gunwale . . . my canoe-bottom . . . my prow . . . my rib . . . my threading-stick . . . my prow-board . . . my transverse stick . . . my canoe-side." Malinowski diagrams the garden site as a square piece of land subdivided into squares; the Trobrianders refer to it in the same terms as those which they use in referring to a village—a bulky object or an aggregate of bumps. When the plots in the garden site are apportioned to the gardeners, the named plots are assigned by name, the others by location along each named side of the garden. After this, the inner plots, the "belly" of the garden, are apportioned. Following along a physical rim is a procedure we find elsewhere also. In a spell naming villages on the main island, there is a long list of villages that lie along the coast northward, then westward around the island, then south. To us, of course, this is lineal order. But we have no indication that the Trobrianders see other than geographical location, point after point, as they move over a physically continuous area; the line as a guide to procedure is not necessarily implied. No terms are used here that might be taken as an implication of continuity: no "along the coast" or "around" or "northward."

Line vs. Pattern

When we in our culture deal with events or experiences of the self, we use the line as guide for various reasons, two of which I shall take up here. First, we feel we must arrange events chronologically in a lineal order; how else could our historians discover the causes of a war or a revolution or a defeat? Among the Trobrianders, what corresponds to our history is an aggregate of anecdotes, that is, unconnected points, told without respect to chronological sequence, or development, or casual relationship; with no grammatical distinction made between words referring to past events, or to present or contemplated ones. And in telling an anecdote, they take no care that a temporal sequence should be followed. For instance, they said to Malinowski: "They-eat-taro, they-spew-taro, they-disgusted-taro"; but if time, as we believe, is a moving line, then the revulsion came first in time, the vomiting was the result, coming afterward. Again, they say, "This-here . . . ripes . . . falls-down truly gives-birth . . . sits seed in belly-his"; but certainly the seed is there first, and the birth follows in time, if time is lineal.

Secondly, we arrange events and objects in a sequence that is climactic, in size and intensity, in emotional meaning, or according to some other principle. We often arrange events from earlier to later, not because we are interested in historical causation, but because the present is the climax of our history. But when the Trobriander relates happenings, there is no developmental arrangement, no building up of emotional tone. His stories have no plot, no lineal development, no climax. And when he repeats his garden spell, his list is neither climactic nor anti-climactic; it sounds merely untidy to us:

> The belly of my garden lifts.
> The belly of my garden rises.
> The belly of my garden reclines.
> The belly of my garden is-a-bushhen's-nest-in-lifting.
> The belly of my garden is-an-anthill.

The belly of my garden lifts-bends.
The belly of my garden is-an-ironwood-tree-in-lifting.
The belly of my garden lies-down.
The belly of my garden burgeons.

When the Trobrianders set out on their great ceremonial kula expedition, they follow a pre-established order. First comes the canoe of the Tolabwaga, an obscure subclan. Next come the canoes of the great chiefs. But this is not climactic; after the great chiefs come the commoners. The order derives meaning, not from lineal sequence, but from correspondence with a present, experienced, meaningful pattern, which is the re-creation or realization of the mythical pattern: that which has been ordained of old and is forever. Its meaning does not lie in an item-to-item relationship, but in fitness, in the repetition of an established unit.

An ordering of this sort gives members of our society a certain aesthetic disphoria except when, through deliberate training, we learn to go beyond our cultural expectation or when we are too young to have taken on the phrasings of our culture. When we manipulate objects naively, we arrange them on some climactic lineal principle. Think of a college commencement, with the faculty arranged in order of rank or length of tenure or other mark of importance; with the students arranged according to increasing physical height, from shortest to tallest, actually the one absolutely irrelevant principle as regards the completion of their college education, which is the occasion for the celebration. Even when the sophisticated avoid this principle, they are not unconscious of it; they are deliberately avoiding something that is there.

And our arrangement of history, when we ourselves are personally involved, is mainly climactic. My great grandmother sewed by candlelight, my grandmother used a kerosene lamp, my mother did her studying by gaslight, I did it by a naked electric ceiling light, and my children have diffused fluorescent lighting. This is progress; this is the meaningful sequence. To the Trobriander, climax in history is abominable, a denial of all good, since it would imply not only that change is present but also that change increases the good; but to him value lies in sameness, in repeated pattern, in the incorporation of all time within the same point. What is good in life is exact identity with all past Trobriand experience, and all mythical experience. There is no boundary between past Trobriand existence and the present; he can indicate that an action is completed, but this does not mean that the action is past; it may be completed and present or timeless. Where we would say "many years ago" and use the past tense, the Trobriander says "in my father's childhood" and uses nontemporal verbs; he places the event situationally, not temporally. Past, present, and future are presented linguistically as the same, are present in his existence; and sameness with what we call the past and with myth represents value to the Trobriander. Where we see a developmental line, the Trobriander sees a point—at most, swelling in value. Where we find pleasure and satisfaction in moving away from the point, in change as variety or progress, the Trobriander finds it in the repetition of the known, in maintaining the point: that is, in what we call monotony. Aesthetic validity, dignity, and value come to him, not through arrangement into a climactic line, but rather in the undisturbed incorporation of the events within their original, nonlineal order. The only history that has meaning for him is that which evokes the value of the point or which, in the repetition, swells the value of the point. For example, every occasion in which akula object participates becomes an ingredient of its being and swells its value; all these occasions are enumerated with great satisfaction, but the lineal course of the traveling kula object is not important.

As we see our history climactically, so do we plan future experiences climactically, leading up to future satisfaction or meaning. Who but a very young child would think of starting a meal with strawberry shortcake and ending it with spinach? We have come to identify the end of the meal with the height of satisfaction, and we identify semantically the words *dessert* and *reward*, only because of the similarity of their positions in a climactic line. The Trobriand meal has no dessert, no lone, no climax. The special bit, the relish, is eaten *with* the staple food; it is not something to "look *forward to*," while disposing of a meaningless staple.

None of the Trobriand activities are fitted into a climactic line. There is no job, no labor, no drudgery that finds its reward outside the act. All work contains its own satisfaction. We cannot speak of S—R (stimulus—response) here, as all action contains its own immanent "stimulus." The present is not a means to future satisfaction, but good in itself, as the future is also good in itself: neither better nor worse, neither climactic nor anticlimactic, in fact, not lineally connected nor removed. It follows that the present is not evaluated in terms of its place within a course of action leading upward to a worthy end. In our culture, we can rarely evaluate the present in itself. I tell you that Sally is selling notions at Woolworth's, but this in itself means nothing. It acquires some meaning when I add that she has recently graduated from Vassar. However, I go on to tell you that she has been assistant editor of *Vogue*, next a nursemaid, a charwoman, a public school teacher. But this is mere jumble; it makes no sense and has no meaning, because the series leads to nothing. You cannot relate one job to another, and you are unable to see them discretely simply as part of her being. However, I now add that she is gathering material for a book on the working mother. Now all this falls in line, it makes sense in terms of a career. Now her job is good and it makes her happy, because it is part of a planned climactic line leading to more pay, increased recognition, higher rank. There was a story in a magazine about the college girl who fell in love with the milkman one summer; the reader felt tense until it was discovered that this was just a summer job, that it was only a means for the continuation of the man's education in the Columbia Law School. Our evaluation of happiness and unhappiness is bound with this motion along an envisioned line leading to a desired end. In the fulfillment of this course or career—not in the fulfillment of the self as point—do we find value. Our conception of freedom rests on the principle of noninterference with this moving line, noninterruption of the intended course of action.

It is difficult to tell whether climax is given in experience at all, or whether it is always imposed on the given. At a time when progress and evolution were assumed to be implicit in nature, our musicians and writers gave us climactic works.

Nowadays, our more reflective art does not present experience climactically. Then, is emotion itself climactic? Climax, for us, evokes "thrill" or "drama." But we have cultures, like the Tikopia, where life is lived on an even, emotive plane without thrill or climax. Experiences that "we know to be" climactic are described without climax by them. For example, they, as well as the Trobrianders, described intercourse as an aggregate of pleasurable experiences. But Malinowski is disturbed by this; he cannot place the erotic kiss in Trobriand experience, since it has no climactic function. Again, in our culture, childbearing is climactic. Pregnancy is represented by the usual obstetrician as an uncomfortable means to a dramatic end. For most women, all intensity of natural physical experience is nowadays removed from the actual birth itself; but the approach of birth nevertheless is a period of mounting tension, and drama is supplied by the intensive social recognition of the event, the dramatic accumulation of gifts, flowers, telegrams. A pregnancy is not formally announced, since, if it does not eventuate in birth, it has failed to achieve its end; and failure to reach the climax brings shame. In its later stages, it may be marked with a shower; but the shower looks forward to the birth, it does not celebrate the pregnancy itself. Among the Trobrianders, pregnancy has meaning in itself as a state of being. At a first pregnancy, there is a long ceremonial involving "preparatory" work on the part of many people, which merely celebrates the pregnancy. It does not anchor the baby; it does not have *as its purpose* a more comfortable time during the pregnancy; it does not *lead* to an easier birth or a healthy baby. It makes the woman's skin white and makes her be at her most beautiful; yet this *leads* to nothing, since she must not attract men, not even her own husband.

Conclusion

Are we then right in accepting without question the presence of a line in reality? Are we in a position to say with assurance that the Trobrianders are wrong and we are right? Much of our present-day thinking and much of our evaluation are based on the premise of the line and of the line as good. Students have been refused admittance to college because the autobiographic sketches accompanying their applications showed absence of the line; they lacked purposefulness and ability to plan; they were inadequate as to character as well as intellectually. Our conception of personality formation, our stress on the significance of success and failure and of frustration in general, is based on the axiomatically postulated line. How can there be blocking without pre-supposed lineal motion or effort? If I walk along a path because I like the country, or if it is not important to get to a particular point at a particular time, then the insuperable puddle from the morning's shower is not frustrating; I throw stones into it and watch the ripples, and then choose another path. If the undertaking is of value in itself, a point good in itself and not because it leads to something, then failure has no symbolic meaning; it merely results in no cake for supper, or less money in the family budget; it is not personally destructive. But failure is devastating in our culture, because it is not failure of the undertaking alone; it is the moving, becoming, lineally conceived self that has failed.

Ethnographers have occasionally remarked that the people whom they studied showed no annoyance when interrupted. Is this an indication of mild temper, or might it be the case that they were not interrupted at all, as there was no expectation of lineal continuity? Such questions are new in anthropology, and most ethnographers therefore never thought of recording material that would answer them. However, we do have enough material to make us question the line as basic to all experience; whether it is actually present in given reality or not, it is not always present in experienced reality. We cannot even take it for granted as existing among those members of our society who are not completely or naively steeped in their culture— among many of our artists, for example. And we should be very careful, in studying other cultures, to avoid the unexamined assumption that their actions are based on the prediction of a lineal reality.

COMMENTS ON "LINEAL AND NONLINEAL

CODIFICATIONS OF REALITY"

Robert Graves

When discussing differences between the sound-complexes applied in various countries to the same reality, one should first make sure that it *is* the same reality. The words *brot, pain,* and *pan* are given only one meaning in an English polyglot dictionary: namely, "bread." But heavy German *brot,* and light French *pain,* and hard Spanish *pan* are not at all the same reality. The different words used in these three countries for parliament, or for smuggling, are likewise given only one meaning in the English polyglot dictionary. Yet public attitudes toward parliament, or toward smuggling, vary so greatly between Germany, France, and Spain that one cannot equate the realities without doing violence to national history.

When a Spaniard comes home from a visit to Germany, he describes *brot* as *"unespecie de pan"* and the Reichstag as *"un poco como las Cortes nuestras."* He does not perceive the same reality; because it is not the same. As for *geld, argent,* and *dinero,* translated in English as "money," the physical reality of money and the national attitudes toward it also vary enormously.

I doubt whether Mrs. Lee has pondered sufficiently on the metaphorical use of "sister" in English. It does not merely mean "a female who has one or both physical parents in common with one or more males or females." Sometimes it corresponds with the term *kainga* ("joking relatives") in Otong Javanese: for example, in "sisters of the trapeze," "the Press sisterhood," "sisterly teasing." Sometimes it corresponds with the term *ave,* where there is "formality, prohibition, strain," and vulgar jokes are barred: as when a hospital nurse is called "Sister," or a preacher addresses his "sisters in Christ."

Nor does the English language seem to work on very different principles from the Wintu Indian dialect here mentioned. The Wintu word *poq* corresponds closely with the English "peg," and may indeed be a borrowing from it.

1) I pegged the guy-ropes down.
2) "I seen him a-crouching on one peg."
3) Birds are pegging merrily along the snow toward breadcrumbs.
4) "Peg-top mushrooms, that's what we call 'em here."
5) You walk peg-leggedly ahead of me.

And in English it is not unusual to give different names to growing things as descriptions of the stages they have reached. The Trobriander may call a yam a *taytu*, or a *yowana*, or a *silasata*, or something else according to its size and maturity; but the English huntsman has several distinct terms for a stag as it develops from a fawn to a hart-royal; and the fisherman has another range of precise terms for the growing salmon—*alevin, parr, smolt, grilse, kelt, salmon*.

Notions of linear direction, labors planned, courses reckoned, toils rewarded, are fostered by a cold climate and by the difficulty of agriculture and fuel gathering. In many Pacific islands, a generation or two ago, where the natives could live for nothing with a minimum of effort, and needed go nowhere except for fun, purposiveness was pretty well at a discount once social conventions of mutual help and toleration had been established. Nobody felt called upon to think of the past or plan for the future. Fishing was fun, and when a family grew tired of yams and pork, someone said: "Let's fish!" So they went to fish. As W. H. R. Rivers noted in one Melanesian island—I forget which —no particular man took charge of the expedition, none decided who would steer the course (the softest option), or who would take the bow paddle, but everything sorted itself out naturally and without argument, by group impulse. There were hereditary functions and duties, of course, but these merely served to make individual decisions or directives unnecessary. Western traders have had trouble in contending with such lack of purposiveness: if they are to get regular supplies of copra they must create needs and ambitions and thus teach the natives how to plan and organize.

This problem has not been easy to solve, even with bribes of gin, toys, and cinema shows. English-speaking children on holiday, freed of duties and worries, also make a cult of purpose-lessness, which often infuriates their parents. "Why don't you do something useful?" we ask, and can induce them to do something useful only by taking the trader's way; except that we provide ice cream instead of gin. At English-speaking schools, games are the children's main recreation, and until a few generations ago, when they were made compulsory and were organized by masters and monitors, they played for the sake of the game, as the Trobrianders do, in theory at least. Today, however, pro-fessionalism is encouraged early, and children play for glory rather than fun.

When a little boy, I used to go out walking without any particular aim, but that phase soon passed, as a result of purpose-ful family conditioning, into one of deliberate outings to see something or bring something home. Purposefulness is not in-sisted upon quite so severely in Mediterranean countries as in Northern Europe; people live with less effort, and so tend to wander aimlessly about. Yet it is a difficult feat for a conditioned Englishman to go in no particular direction. I wrote about this once:

IN NO DIRECTION

To go in no direction
  Surely as carelessly,
Walking on the hills alone,
  I never found easy.

Either I sent leaf or stick
  Twirling in the air,
Whose fall might be prophetic,
  Pointing 'there',

Or in superstition
  Edged somewhat away
From a sure direction,
  Yet could not stray.

Or undertook the climb
That I had avoided
Directionless some other time,
Or had not avoided,

Or called as companion
Some eyeless ghost
And held his no direction
Till my feet were lost.

The tyranny of the directive line cannot, however, be a very ancient one, to judge from the words that convey linearity. "Line" in English is the Latin *linea*, which originally meant the taut linen thread hanging from the spindle, and was innocent of lateral direction. The Greek for "straight," *orthos*, orginally meant "rising upright from a recumbent posture"—only later did it convey lateral extent. "Circle" in English is *circulum* in Latin, an onomatopoeic borrowing from the *kirk-kirk* noise made by a falcon (*kirke* in Greek) as it wheels through a lazy spiral. The Greek *kuklos* ("circle") is another form of the same word. "Circle" was later applied, by analogy, to the directed circling of a blindfold ox or ass in a mill, and so to the circular track its hoofs made.

The economy of straight lines in agriculture became evident when the plough displaced the mattock; the value of straight lines in warfare became evident when the tactics of locked shields and short stabbing-swords displaced individual target and broad-sword fighting, and when straight military roads, radiating from the national capital, made it possible to defend threatened points of the frontier at speed and in considerable force. Admittedly, straight ploughing has since proved a curse to agriculture by its creation of dust bowls; and linear military thinking has proved a curse when countered by the nonlinear tactics of infiltration; also, the ordering of people and things on linear principles has made for a deal of unnecessary human misery.

"Nature abhors a straight line." A lineally organized engineer-friend from New Zealand once criticized the wasteful architecture of an old cottage in which I lived: plumb line, level, and T-square would have reduced its building costs by a quarter, he remarked. I answered in his own language that the work-efficiency of the occupants must be taken into financial consideration. I mentioned recent experiments in factory workers' fatigue reaction to straight lines, and the high incidence of nervous hysteria in housing estates where, for economy's sake, identical houses line parallel streets, and no irregularities relieve the eye. That, I said, may explain why, as a rule, cottage homes are kept neat but housing-estate homes tend to be untidy.

Trobrianders do not insist on sexual activity as the cause of procreation, though aware of it as a needful antecedent. But this attitude conveniently (and, I think, purposefully) separates two very different concepts: erotic love and parenthood. In Melanesia, premarital intercourse is legitimized, and, owing to certain natural prophylactic precautions, girls very rarely become pregnant before choosing husbands. Officially, in Western civilization, premarital intercourse ranks as a sin, and even marital intercourse is frowned upon by some churches unless for the purpose of procreation. Only since the spread of artificial contraceptive methods has the Melanesian system, so abhorrent to Victorian missionaries (as the similar Canaanite system was to the Hebrew prophets), been tacitly accepted in the larger cities of England and North America. Premarital intercourse, once freed from anxiety about possible impregnation, now seems a sensible means of discovering one's sexual needs or dislikes: the lover being a lover, not a possible father.

This leads to a consideration of the Trobrianders' disgust with amorous favors given in hope of reward, or with the giving of any gift in the hope of another as good or better. No such disgust is expressed by the more commercial representatives of Western civilization, for whom "everything has its price," though felt strongly enough in so-called "decent society." It is implicit in such opprobrious terms as "cupboard love," "gold digger," and "calculated generosity," which are used wherever the relationship, it is felt, should not be regarded as a commercial one. The commercial principle seems far seldomer applied to work in Europe than in North America, where craftsmanship (the theory that one works for the sake of doing a particular job well) has long been displaced by enterprise (the theory that one works to make money, without taking any particular interest in the goods produced.) Britain's present commercial instability may, in part, be caused by a reluctance to regard craftsmanship as the luxury that Americans have agreed to make it.

Reward as a climax to labor is naturally emphasized in regions where bread does not grow on trees and must be produced by a long sequence of difficult agricultural operations; but it can hardly be disregarded even among Trobrianders when they come home hungry from a successful fishing expedition and expect a suitable celebration. And Mrs. Lee's notion that all Westerners look forward to dessert is surely a fallacy. Most women may; most children certainly do; but most men are chiefly interested in the roast, as were Homer's heroes. Etymologically, *dessert* does not mean "that which has been deserved"; on the contrary, it means *trivia,* the apples and nuts brought to table after the main dish has been *desservi,* or removed. For men, the important sweet is the currant jelly, which goes with the mutton, or the cranberry jelly, which goes with the turkey, or the apple sauce, which goes with the pork.

Western notions of reward as a climax have encouraged thrift, thus benefiting banks and insurance companies, and, when this climax can safely be postponed to "Heaven," have allowed greedy employers to exploit their wage slaves. Yet today, in Europe, the reward climax is no longer quite so valid as it used to be. The virtue of thrift is passing: sensible people will eat the best breakfast they can afford to help them through a day's work. They reckon that they might otherwise be too tired to eat at all when returning home for supper. It was Samuel Butler, the leading 20th century modernist, who noted that sensible people always eat a bunch of grapes downward, the big ones first. He added that if the hangover preceded the delights of intoxication, drunkenness would be a Christian virtue.

It may well be that in America, when asked to describe a person, people follow an imaginary line, usually downward. In England, we go straight for the salient features: "big man with a limp, red nose, rimless glasses, big belly, dirty complexion, pudgy hands, rheumy eyes, not much hair." Nor, if challenged to name all the English counties with their capitals do we follow a downward line, unless we have once learned them by rote at school. Myself, I would remember only the first three on the list: Northumberland, Newcastle-upon-Tyne; Durham, Durham on the Weir; Yorkshire, York on the Ouse. After that, I should behave like a Trobriander: naming Lancashire as Yorkshire's rival; next, Staffordshire, another leading industrial county; then remember Derbyshire to the north; then turn by contrast to the sleepy, relatively unspoiled counties of Somerset, Dorset, Devon, and Cornwall; then switch over to East Anglia for a breath of east wind, or go back north, to pick up Westmoreland and Cumberland—and so on. Incidentally, none of our counties have straight borders, as most American and Canadian states have; and few of our roads run straight, so linear memory is not encouraged.

Mrs. Lee seems to be mistaken in suggesting that when a Trobriander relates happenings "there is no developmental arrangement, no building up of emotional tone . . . no plot, no lineal development, no climax—unless Malinowski has hideously deceived us with his Legend of *Inuvayla'u,* too bawdy a story to repeat here, which has perfect development: Inuvayla'u's seductions, the anger of the people, his self-castration, his sad departure from the island, his wistful return, his gentle end. And there is one side of island life in which, according to Malinowski, the Trobriander can be regarded as extremely purposive: the erotic side. He often uses games, especially hide and seek and the tug of war, as an excuse for making passes at women, and spends a great deal of time working on magical spells to win himself reluctant maidenheads. The girls who take part in organized and licensed sexual raids on the young men of neighboring villages are, in theory, going merely for fun; but, Malinowski writes, the underlying reason is often said to be that their store of betel-nut, tobacco, and personal jewelry needs replenishment in the form of love-gifts.

THE NEW LANGUAGES

Edmund Carpenter

> *Brain of the New World,*
> *What a task is thine,*
> *To formulate the modern*
> *. . . to recast poems, churches, art*
> WHITMAN

English is a mass medium. All languages are mass media. The new mass media—film, radio, TV—are new languages, their grammars as yet unknown. Each codifies reality differently; each conceals a unique metaphysics. Linguists tell us it's possible to say anything in any language if you use enough words or images, but there's rarely time; the natural course is for a culture to exploit its media biases.

Writing, for example, didn't record oral language; it was a new language, which the spoken word came to imitate. Writing encouraged an analytical mode of thinking with emphasis upon lineality. Oral languages tended to be polysynthetic, composed of great, tight conglomerates, like twisted knots, within which images were juxtaposed, inseparably fused; written communications consisted of little words chronologically ordered. Subject became distinct from verb, adjective from noun, thus separating actor from action, essence from form. Where preliterate man imposed form diffidently, temporarily—for such transitory forms lived but temporarily on the tip of his tongue, in the living situation—the printed word was inflexible, permanent, in touch with eternity: it embalmed truth for posterity.

This embalming process froze language, eliminated the art of ambiguity, made puns "the lowest form of wit," destroyed word linkages. The word became a static symbol, applicable to and separate from that which it symbolized. It now belonged to the objective world; it could be seen. Now came the distinction between being and meaning, the dispute as to whether the Eucharist *was* or only *signified* the body of the Sacrifice. The word became a neutral symbol, no longer an inextricable part of a creative process.

Gutenberg completed the process. The manuscript page with pictures, colors, correlation between symbol and space, gave way to uniform type, the black-and-white page, read silently, alone. The format of the book favored lineal expression, for the argument ran like a thread from cover to cover: subject to verb to object, sentence to sentence, paragraph to paragraph, chapter to chapter, carefully structured from beginning to end, with value embedded in the climax. This was not true of great poetry and drama, which retained multi-perspective, but it was true of most books, particularly texts, histories, autobiographies, novels. Events were arranged chronologically and hence, it was assumed, causally; relationship, not being, was valued. The author became an *authority;* his data were serious, that is, *serially* organized. Such data, if sequentially ordered and printed, conveyed value and truth; arranged any other way, they were suspect.

The newspaper format brought an end to book culture. It offers short, discrete articles that give important facts first and then taper off to incidental details, which may be, and often are, eliminated by the make-up man. The fact that reporters cannot control the length of their articles means that, in writing them, emphasis can't be placed on structure, at least in the traditional linear sense, with climax or conclusion at the end. Everything has to be captured in the headline; from there it goes down the pyramid to incidentals. In fact there is often more in the headline than in the article; occasionally, no article at all accompanies the banner headline.

The position and size of articles on the front page are determined by interest and importance, not content. Unrelated reports from Moscow, Sarawak, London, and Ittipik are juxtaposed; time and space, as separate concepts, are destroyed and the *here* and *now* presented as a single Gestalt. Subway readers consume everything on the front page, then turn to page 2 to read, in incidental order, continuations. A Toronto banner headline ran: TOWNSEND TO MARRY PRINCESS; directly beneath this was a second headline: *Fabian Says This May Not Be Sex Crime*. This went unnoticed by eyes and minds conditioned to consider each newspaper item in isolation.

Such a format lends itself to simultaneity, not chronology or lineality. Items abstracted from a total situation aren't arranged in casual sequence, but presented holistically, as raw experience. The front page is a cosmic *Finnegans Wake*.

The disorder of the newspaper throws the reader into a producer role. The reader has to process the news himself; he has to co-create, to cooperate in the creation of the work. The newspaper format calls for the direct participation of the consumer.

In magazines, where a writer more frequently controls the length of his article, he can, if he wishes, organize it in traditional style, but the majority don't. An increasingly popular presentation is the printed symposium, which is little more than collected opinions, pro and con. The magazine format as a whole opposes lineality; its pictures lack tenses. In *Life*, extremes are juxtaposed: space ships and prehistoric monsters, Flemish monasteries and dope addicts. It creates a sense of urgency and uncertainty: the next page is unpredictable. One encounters rapidly a riot in Teheran, a Hollywood marriage, the wonders of the Eisenhower administration, a two-headed calf, a party on Jones beach, all sandwiched between ads. The eye takes in the page as a whole (readers may pretend this isn't so, but the success of advertising suggests it is), and the page—indeed, the whole magazine—becomes a single Gestalt where association, though not causal, is often lifelike.

The same is true of the other new languages. Both radio and TV offer short, unrelated programs, interrupted between and within by commercials. I say "interrupted," being myself an anachronism of book culture, but my children don't regard them as interruptions, as breaking continuity. Rather, they regard them as part of a whole, and their reaction is neither one of annoyance nor one of indifference. The ideal news broadcast has half a dozen speakers from as many parts of the world on as many subjects. The London correspondent doesn't comment on what the Washington correspondent has just said; he hasn't even heard him.

The child is right in not regarding commercials as interruptions. For the only time anyone smiles on TV is in commercials. The rest of life, in news broadcasts and soap operas, is presented as so horrible that the only way to get through life is to buy this product: then you'll smile. Aesop never wrote a clearer fable. It's heaven and hell brought up to date: Hell in the headline, Heaven in the ad. Without the other, neither has meaning.

There's pattern in these new media—not line, but knot; not lineality or causality or chronology, nothing that leads to a desired climax; but a Gordian knot without antecedents or results, containing within itself carefully selected elements, juxtaposed, inseparably fused; a knot that can't be untied to give the long, thin cord of lineality.

This is especially true of ads that never present an ordered, sequential, rational argument but simply present the product associated with desirable things or attitudes. Thus Coca-Cola is shown held by a beautiful blonde, who sits in a Cadillac, surrounded by bronze, muscular admirers, with the sun shining overhead. By repetition these elements become associated, in our minds, into a pattern of sufficient cohesion so that one element can magically evoke the others. If we think of ads as designed solely to sell products, we miss their main effect: to increase pleasure in the consumption of the product. Coca-Cola is far more than a cooling drink; the consumer participates, vicariously, in a much larger experience. In Africa, in Melanesia, to drink a Coke is to participate in the American way of life.

Of the new languages, TV comes closest to drama and ritual. It combines music and art, language and gesture, rhetoric and color. It favors simultaneity of visual and auditory images. Cameras focus not on speakers but on persons spoken to or about; the audience *hears* the accuser but *watches* the accused. In a single impression it hears the prosecutor, watches the trembling hands of the big-town crook, and sees the look of moral indignation on Senator Tobey's face. This is real drama, in process, with the outcome uncertain. Print can't do this; it has a different bias.

Books and movies only pretend uncertainty, but live TV retains this vital aspect of life. Seen on TV, the fire in the 1952 Democratic Convention threatened briefly to become a conflagration; seen on newsreel, it was history, without potentiality.

The absence of uncertainty is no handicap to other media, if they are properly used, for their biases are different. Thus it's clear from the beginning that Hamlet is a doomed man, but, far from detracting in interest, this heightens the sense of tragedy.

Now, one of the results of the time-space duality that developed in Western culture, principally from the Renaissance on, was a separation within the arts. Music, which created symbols in time, and graphic art, which created symbols in space, became separate pursuits, and men gifted in one rarely pursued the other. Dance and ritual, which inherently combined them, fell in popularity. Only in drama did they remain united.

It is significant that of the four new media, the three most recent are dramatic media, particularly TV, which combines language, music, art, dance. They don't, however, exercise the same freedom with time that the stage dares practice. An intricate plot, employing flash backs, multiple time perspectives and overlays, intelligible on the stage, would mystify on the screen. The audience has no time to think back, to establish relations between early hints and subsequent discoveries. The picture passes before the eyes too quickly; there are no intervals in which to take stock of what has happened and make conjectures of what is going to happen. The observer is in a more passive state, less interested in subtleties. Both TV and film are nearer to narrative and depend much more upon the episodic. An intricate time construction can be done in film, but in fact rarely is. The soliloquies of *Richard III* belong on the stage; the film audience was unprepared for them. On stage Ophelia's death was described by three separate groups: one hears the announcement and watches the reactions simultaneously. On film the camera flatly shows her drowned where "a willow lies aslant a brook."

Media differences such as these mean that it's not simply a

question of communicating a single idea in different ways but that a given idea or insight belongs primarily, though not exclusively, to one medium, and can be gained or communicated best through that medium.

Thus the book was ideally suited for discussing evolution and progress. Both belonged, almost exclusively, to book culture. Like a book, the idea of progress was an abstracting, organizing principle for the interpretation and comprehension of the incredibly complicated record of human experience. The sequence of events was believed to have a direction, to follow a given course along an axis of time; it was held that civilization, like the reader's eye (in J. B. Bury's words), "has moved, is moving, and will move in a desirable direction. Knowledge will advance, and with that advance, reason and decency must increasingly prevail among men." Here we see the three main elements of book lineality: the line, the point moving along that line, and its movement toward a desirable goal.

The Western conception of a definite moment in the present, of the present as a definite moment or a definite point, so important in book-dominated languages, is absent, to my knowledge, in oral languages. Absent as well, in oral societies, are such animating and controlling ideas as Western individualism and three-dimensional perspective, both related to this conception of the definite moment, and both nourished, probably bred, by book culture.

Each medium selects its ideas. TV is a tiny box into which people are crowded and must live; film gives us the wide world. With its huge screen, film is perfectly suited for social drama, Civil War panoramas, the sea, land erosion, Cecil B. DeMille spectaculars. In contrast, the TV screen has room for two, at the most three, faces, comfortably. TV is closer to stage, yet different. Paddy Chayefsky writes:

The theatre audience is far away from the actual action of the drama. They cannot see the silent reactions of the players. They must be told in a loud voice what is going on. The plot movement from one scene to another must be marked, rather than gently shaded as is required in television. In television, however, you can dig into the most humble, ordinary relationships; the relationship of bourgeois children to their mother, of middle-class husband to his wife, of white-collar father to his secretary—in short, the relationships of the people. We relate to each other in an incredibly complicated manner. There is far more exciting drama in the reasons why a man gets married than in why he murders someone. The man who is unhappy in his job, the wife who thinks of a lover, the girl who wants to get into television, your father, your mother, sister, brothers, cousins, friends—all these are better subjects for drama than Iago. What makes a man ambitious? Why does a girl always try to steal her kid sister's boy friends? Why does your uncle attend his annual class reunion faithfully every year? Why do you always find it depressing to visit your father? These are the substances of good television drama; and the deeper you probe into and examine the twisted, semi-formed complexes of emotional entanglements, the more exciting your writing becomes.[1]

This is the primary reason, I believe, why Greek drama is more readily adapted to TV than to film. The boxed-in quality of live TV lends itself to static literary tragedy with greater ease than does the elastic, energetic, expandable movie. Guthrie's recent movie of *Oedipus* favored the panoramic shot rather than the selective eye. It consisted of a succession of tableaux, a series of elaborate, unnatural poses. The effect was of congested groups of people moving in tight formation as though they had trained for it by living for days together in a self-service elevator. With the lines, "I grieve for the City, and for myself and you . . . and walk through endless ways of thought," the inexorable tragedy moved to its horrible "come to realize" climax as though everyone were stepping on everyone else's feet.

The tight, necessary conventions of live TV were more sympathetic to Sophocles in the Aluminium Hour's *Antigone*. Restrictions of space are imposed on TV as on the Greek stage by the size and inflexibility of the studio. Squeezed by physical limitations, the producer was forced to expand the viewer's imagination with ingenious devices.

When T. S. Eliot adapted *Murder in the Cathedral* for film, he noted a difference in realism between cinema and stage:

Cinema, even where fantasy is introduced, is much more realistic than the stage. Especially in an historical picture, the setting, the costume, and the way of life represented have to be

[1] *Television Plays,* New York, Simon and Schuster, 1955, pp. 176-78.

accurate. Even a minor anachronism is intolerable. On the stage much more can be overlooked or forgiven; and indeed, an excessive care for accuracy of historical detail can become burdensome and distracting. In watching a stage performance, the member of the audience is in direct contact with the actor playing a part. In looking at a film, we are much more passive; as audience, we contribute less. We are seized with the illusion that we are observing an actual event, or at least a series of photographs of the actual event; and nothing must be allowed to break this illusion. Hence the precise attention to detail.[2]

If two men are on a stage in a theatre, the dramatist is obliged to motivate their presence; he has to account for their existing on the stage at all. Whereas if a camera is following a figure down a street or is turned to any object whatever, there is no need for a reason to be provided. Its grammar contains that power of statement of motivation, no matter what it looks at.

In the theatre, the spectator sees the enacted scene as a whole in space, always seeing the whole of the space. The stage may present only one corner of a large hall, but that corner is always totally visible all through the scene. And the spectator always sees that scene from a fixed, unchanging distance and from an angle of vision that doesn't change. Perspective may change from scene to scene, but within one scene it remains constant. Distance never varies.

But in film and TV, distance and angle constantly shift. The same scene is shown in multiple perspective and focus. The viewer sees it from here, there, then over here; finally he is drawn inexorably into it, becomes part of it. He ceases to be a spectator. Balázs writes:

Although we sit in our seats, we do not see Romeo and Juliet from there. We look up into Juliet's balcony with Romeo's eyes and look down on Romeo with Juliet's. Our eye and with it our consciousness is identified with the characters in the film, we look at the world out of their eyes and have no angle of vision of our own. We walk amid crowds, ride, fly or fall with the hero and if one character looks into the other's eyes, he looks into our eyes from the screen, for, our eyes are in the camera and become identical with the gaze of the characters. They see with our

[2] George Hoellering and T. S. Eliot, *Film of Murder in the Cathedral,* New York, Harcourt, Brace & Co., 1952, p. vi; London, Faber & Faber, 1952.

eyes. Herein lies the psychological act of identification. Nothing like this "identification" has ever occurred as the effect of any other system of art and it is here that the film manifests its absolute artistic novelty.

. . . Not only can we see, in the isolated "shots" of a scene, the very atoms of life and their innermost secrets revealed at close quarters, but we can do so without any of the intimate secrecy being lost, as always happens in the exposure of a stage performance or of a painting. The new theme which the new means of expression of film art revealed was not a hurricane at sea or the eruption of a volcano: it was perhaps a solitary tear slowly welling up in the corner of a human eye.

. . . Not to speak does not mean that one has nothing to say. Those who do not speak may be brimming over with emotions which can be expressed only in forms and pictures, in gesture and play of feature. The man of visual culture uses these not as substitutes for words, as a deaf-mute uses his fingers.[3]

The gestures of visual man are not intended to convey concepts that can be expressed in words, but inner experiences, nonrational emotions, which would still remain unexpressed when everything that can be told has been told. Such emotions lie in the deepest levels. They cannot be approached by words that are mere reflections of concepts, any more than musical experiences can be expressed in rational concepts. Facial expression is a human experience rendered immediately visible without the intermediary of word. It is Turgenev's "living truth of the human face."

Printing rendered illegible the faces of men. So much could be read from paper that the method of conveying meaning by facial expression fell into desuetude. The press grew to be the main bridge over which the more remote interhuman spiritual exchanges took place; the immediate, the personal, the inner, died. There was no longer need for the subtler means of expression provided by the body. The face became immobile; the inner life, still. Wells that dry up are wells from which no water is dipped.

Just as radio helped bring back inflection in speech, so film and TV are aiding us in the recovery of gesture and facial aware-

---

[3] Béla Balázs, *Theory of Film,* New York, Roy Publishers, 1953, pp. 48, 31, 40; London, Denis Dobson, 1952.

ness—a rich, colorful language, conveying moods and emotions, happenings and characters, even thoughts, none of which could be properly packaged in words. If film had remained silent for another decade, how much faster this change might have been!

Feeding the product of one medium through another medium creates a new product. When Hollywood buys a novel, it buys a title and the publicity associated with it: nothing more. Nor should it.

Each of the four versions of the *Caine Mutiny*—book, play, movie, TV—had a different hero: Willie Keith, the lawyer Greenwald, the United States Navy, and Captain Queeg, respectively. Media and audience biases were clear. Thus the book told, in lengthy detail, of the growth and making of Ensign William Keith, American man, while the movie camera with its colorful shots of ships and sea, unconsciously favored the Navy as hero, a bias supported by the fact the Navy cooperated with the movie makers. Because of stage limitations, the play was confined, except for the last scene, to the courtroom, and favored the defense counsel as hero. The TV show, aimed at a mass audience, emphasized patriotism, authority, allegiance. More important, the cast was reduced to the principals and the plot to its principles; the real moral problem—the refusal of subordinates to assist an incompetent, unpopular superior—was clear, whereas in the book it was lost under detail, in the film under scenery. Finally, the New York play, with its audience slanted toward Expense Account patronage—Mr. Sampson, Western Sales Manager for the Cavity Drill Company—became a morality play with Willie Keith, innocent American youth, torn between two influences: Keefer, clever author but moral cripple, and Greenwald, equally brilliant but reliable, a businessman's intellectual. Greenwald saves Willie's soul.

The film *Moby Dick* was in many ways an improvement on the book, primarily because of its explicitness. For *Moby Dick* is one of those admittedly great classics, like *Robinson Crusoe* or Kafka's *Trial*, whose plot and situation, as distilled apart from the book by time and familiarity, are actually much more imposing than the written book itself. It's the drama of Ahab's defiance rather than Melville's uncharted leviathan meanderings that is the greatness of *Moby Dick*. On film, instead of laborious tacks through leagues of discursive interruptions, the most vivid descriptions of whales and whaling become part of the action. On film, the viewer was constantly aboard ship: each scene an instantaneous shot of whaling life, an effect achieved in the book only by illusion, by constant, detailed reference. From start to finish, all the action of the film served to develop what was most central to the theme—a man's magnificent and blasphemous pride in attempting to destroy the brutal, unreasoning force that maims him and turns man-made order into chaos. Unlike the book, the film gave a spare, hard, compelling dramatization, free of self-conscious symbolism.

Current confusion over the respective roles of the new media comes largely from a misconception of their function. They are art-forms, not substitutes for human contact. Insofar as they attempt to usurp speech and personal, living relations, they harm. This, of course, has long been one of the problems of book culture, at least during the time of its monopoly of Western middle-class thought. But this was never a legitimate function of books, nor of any other medium. Whenever a medium goes claim jumping, trying to work areas where it is ill-suited, conflicts occur with other media, or, more accurately, between the vested interests controlling each. But, when media simply exploit their own formats, they become complementary and cross-fertile.

Some people who have no one around talk to cats, and you can hear their voices in the next room, and they sound silly, because the cat won't answer, but that suffices to maintain the illusion that their world is made up of living people, while it is not. Mechanized mass media reverse this: now mechanical cats talk to humans. There's no genuine feedback.

This charge is often leveled by academicians at the new media, but it holds equally for print. The open-mouthed, glaze-eyed TV spectator is merely the successor of the passive, silent, lonely reader whose head moved back and forth like a shuttle-cock.

When we read, another person thinks for us: we merely repeat his mental process. The greater part of the work of thought is done for us. This is why it relieves us to take up a book after being occupied by our own thoughts. In reading, the mind is only the playground for another's ideas. People who spend most of their lives in reading often lose the capacity for thinking, just as those who always ride forget how to walk. Some people read themselves stupid. Chaplin did a wonderful take-off of this in *City Lights,* when he stood up on a chair to eat the endless confetti that he mistook for spaghetti.

Eliot remarks: "It is often those writers whom we are lucky enough to know whose books we can ignore; and the better we know them personally, the less need we may feel to read what they write."

Frank O'Connor highlights a basic distinction between oral and written traditions: " 'By the hokies, there was a man in this place one time by name of Ned Sullivan, and he had a queer thing happen to him late one night and he coming up the Valley Road from Durlas.' This is how a folk story begins, or should begin. . . . Yet that is how no printed short story should begin, because such a story seems tame when you remove it from its warm nest by the cottage fire, from the sense of an audience with its interjections, and the feeling of terror at what may lurk in the darkness outside."

Face-to-face discourse is not as selective, abstract, nor explicit as any mechanical medium; it probably comes closer to communicating an unabridged situation than any of them, and, insofar as it exploits the give-take of dynamic relationship, it's clearly the most indispensably human one.

Of course, there can be personal involvement in the other media. When Richardson's *Pamela* was serialized in 1741, it aroused such interest that in one English town, upon receipt of the last installment, the church bell announced that virtue had been rewarded. Radio stations have reported receiving quantities of baby clothes and bassinets when, in a soap opera, a heroine had a baby. One of the commonest phrases used by devoted listeners to daytime serials is that they "visited with" Aunt Jenny or Big Sister. BBC and *News Chronicle* report cases of women viewers who kneel before TV sets to kiss male announcers good night.

Each medium, if its bias is properly exploited, reveals and

communicates a unique aspect of reality, of truth. Each offers a different perspective, a way of seeing an otherwise hidden dimension of reality. It's not a question of one reality being true, the others distortions. One allows us to see from here, another from there, a third from still another perspective; taken together they give us a more complete whole, a greater truth. New essentials are brought to the fore, including those made invisible by the "blinders" of old languages.

This is why the preservation of book culture is as important as the development of TV. This is why new languages, instead of destroying old ones, serve as a stimulant to them. Only monopoly is destroyed. When actor-collector Edward G. Robinson was battling actor-collector Vincent Price on art on TV's *$64,000 Challenge,* he was asked how the quiz had affected his life; he answered petulantly, "Instead of looking at the pictures in my art books, I now have to read them." Print, along with all old languages, including speech, has profited enormously from the development of the new media. "The more the arts develop," writes E. M. Forster, "the more they depend on each other for definition. We will borrow from painting first and call it pattern. Later we will borrow from music and call it rhythm."

The appearance of a new medium often frees older media for creative effort. They no longer have to serve the interests of power and profit. Elia Kazan, discussing the American theatre, says:

Take 1900–1920. The theatre flourished all over the country. It had no competition. The box office boomed. The top original fare it had to offer was *The Girl of the Golden West.* Its bow to culture was fusty productions of Shakespeare. . . . Came the moving pictures. The theatre had to be better or go under. It got better. It got so spectacularly better so fast that in 1920–1930 you wouldn't have recognized it. Perhaps it was an accident that Eugene O'Neill appeared at that moment—but it was no accident that in that moment of strange competition, the theatre had room for him. Because it was disrupted and hard pressed, it made room for his experiments, his unheard-of subjects, his passion, his power. There was room for him to grow to his full stature. And there was freedom for the talents that came after his.[4]

[4] "Writers and Motion Pictures," *The Atlantic Monthly,* 199, 1957, p. 69.

Yet a new language is rarely welcomed by the old. The oral tradition distrusted writing, manuscript culture was contemptuous of printing, book culture hated the press, that "slag-heap of hellish passions," as one 19th century scholar called it. A father, protesting to a Boston newspaper about crime and scandal, said he would rather see his children "in their graves while pure in innocence, than dwelling with pleasure upon these reports, which have grown so bold."

What really disturbed book-oriented people wasn't the sensationalism of the newspaper, but its nonlineal format, its nonlineal codifications of experience. The motto of conservative academicians became:*Hold that line!*

A new language lets us see with the fresh, sharp eyes of the child; it offers the pure joy of discovery. I was recently told a story about a Polish couple who, though long resident in Toronto, retained many of the customs of their homeland. Their son despaired of ever getting his father to buy a suit cut in style or getting his mother to take an interest in Canadian life. Then he bought them a TV set, and in a matter of months a major change took place. One evening the mother remarked that "Edith Piaf is the latest thing on Broadway," and the father appeared in "the kind of suit executives wear on TV." For years the father had passed this same suit in store windows and seen it both in advertisements and on living men, but not until he saw it on TV did it become meaningful. This same statement goes for all media: each offers a unique presentation of reality, which when new has a freshness and clarity that is extraordinarily powerful.

This is especially true of TV. We say, "We have a radio" but "We have television"—as if something had happened to us. It's no longer "The skin you love to touch" but "The Nylon that loves to touch you." We don't watch TV; it watches us: it guides us. Magazines and newspapers no longer convey "information" but offer ways of seeing things. They have abandoned realism as too easy: they substitute themselves for realism. *Life* is totally advertisements: its articles package and sell emotions and ideas just as its paid ads sell commodities.

Several years ago, a group of us at the University of Toronto undertook the following experiment: 136 students were divided, on the basis of their over-all academic standing of the previous year, into four equal groups who either (1) heard and saw a lecture delivered in a TV studio, (2) heard and saw this same lecture on a TV screen, (3) heard it over the radio, or (4) read it in manuscript. Thus there were, in the CBC studios, four controlled groups who simultaneously received a single lecture and then immediately wrote an identical examination to test both understanding and retention of content. Later the experiment was repeated, using three similar groups; this time the same lecture was (1) delivered in a classroom, (2) presented as a film (using the kinescope) in a small theatre, and (3) again read in print. The actual mechanics of the experiment were relatively simple, but the problem of writing the script for the lecture led to a consideration of the resources and limitations of the dramatic forms involved.

It immediately became apparent that no matter how the script was written and the show produced, it would be slanted in various ways for and against each of the media involved; no show could be produced that did not contain these biases, and the only real common denominator was the simultaneity of presentation. For each communication channel codifies reality differently and thus influences, to a surprising degree, the content of the message communicated. A medium is not simply an envelope that carries any letter; it is itself a major part of that message. We therefore decided not to exploit the full resources of any one medium, but to try to chart a middle-of-the-road course between all of them.

The lecture that was finally produced dealt with linguistic codifications of reality and metaphysical concepts underlying grammatical systems. It was chosen because it concerned a field in which few students could be expected to have prior knowledge; moreover, it offered opportunities for the use of gesture. The cameras moved throughout the lecture, and took close-ups where relevant. No other visual aids were used, nor were shots taken of the audience while the lecture was in progress. Instead, the cameras simply focused on the speaker for 27 minutes.

The first difference we found between a classroom and a TV lecture was the brevity of the latter. The classroom lecture, if not ideally, at least in practice, sets a slower pace. It's verbose, repetitive. It allows for greater elaboration and permits the lecturer to take up several *related* points. TV, however, is stripped right down; there's less time for qualifications or alternative interpretations and only time enough for *one* point. (Into 27 minutes we put the meat of a two-hour classroom lecture.) The ideal TV speaker states his point and then brings out different facets of it by a variety of illustrations. But the classroom lecturer is less subtle and, to the agony of the better students, repeats and repeats his identical points in the hope, perhaps, that ultimately no student will miss them, or perhaps simply because he is dull. Teachers have had captive audiences for so long that few are equipped to compete for attention via the new media.

The next major difference noted was the abstracting role of each medium, beginning with print. Edmund M. Morgan, Harvard Law Professor, writes:

One who forms his opinion from the reading of any record alone is prone to err, because the printed page fails to produce the impression or convey the idea which the spoken word produced or conveyed. The writer has read charges to the jury which he had previously heard delivered, and has been amazed to see an oral deliverance which indicated a strong bias appear on the printed page as an ideally impartial exposition. He has seen an appellate court solemnly declare the testimony of a witness to be especially clear and convincing which the trial judge had orally characterized as the most abject perjury.[5]

Selectivity of print and radio are perhaps obvious enough, but we are less conscious of it in TV, partly because we have already been conditioned to it by the shorthand of film. Balázs writes:

A man hurries to a railway station to take leave of his beloved. We see him on the platform. We cannot see the train, but the questing eyes of the man show us that his beloved is already seated in the train. We see only a close-up of the man's face, we see it twitch as if startled and then strips of light and shadow, light and shadow flit across it in quickening rhythm.

[5] G. Louis Joughin and Edmund M. Morgan, *The Legacy of Sacco and Vanzetti*, New York, Harcourt, Brace & Co., 1948, p. 34.

Then tears gather in the eyes and that ends the scene. We are expected to know what happened and today we do know, but when I first saw this film in Berlin, I did not at once understand the end of this scene. Soon, however, everyone knew what had happened: the train had started and it was the lamps in its compartment which had thrown their light on the man's face as they glided past ever faster and faster.[6]

As in a movie theatre, only the screen is illuminated, and, on it, only points of immediate relevance are portrayed; everything else is eliminated. This explicitness makes TV not only personal but forceful. That's why stage hands in a TV studio watch the show over floor monitors, rather than watch the actual performance before their eyes.

The script of the lecture, timed for radio, proved too long for TV. Visual aids and gestures on TV not only allow the elimination of certain words, but require a unique script. The ideal radio delivery stresses pitch and intonation to make up for the absence of the visual. That flat, broken speech in "sidewalk interviews" is the speech of a person untrained in radio delivery.

The results of the examination showed that TV had won, followed by lecture, film, radio, and finally print. Eight months later the test was readministered to the bulk of the students who had taken it the first time. Again it was found that there were significant differences between the groups exposed to different media, and these differences were the same as those on the first test, save for the studio group, an uncertain group because of the chaos of the lecture conditions, which had moved from last to second place. Finally, two years later, the experiment was repeated, with major modifications, using students at Ryerson Institute. Marshall McLuhan reports:

In this repeat performance, pains were taken to allow each medium full play of its possibilities with reference to the subject, just as in the earlier experiment each medium was neutralized as much as possible. Only the mimeograph form remained the same in each experiment. Here we added a printed form in which an imaginative typographical layout was followed. The lecturer used the blackboard and permitted discussion. Radio and TV employed dramatization, sound effects and graphics. In the ex-

[6] Béla Balázs, *op. cit.*, pp. 35-36.

amination, radio easily topped TV. Yet, as in the first experiment, both radio and TV manifested a decisive advantage over the lecture and written forms. As a conveyor both of ideas and information, TV was, in this second experiment, apparently enfeebled by the deployment of its dramatic resources, whereas radio benefited from such lavishness. "Technology is explicitness," writes Lyman Bryson. Are both radio and TV more explicit than writing or lecture? Would a greater explicitness, if inherent in these media, account for the ease with which they top other modes of performance? [7]

Announcement of the results of the first experiment evoked considerable interest. Advertising agencies circulated the results with the comment that here, at last, was scientific proof of the superiority of TV. This was unfortunate and missed the main point, for the results didn't indicate the superiority of one medium over others. They merely directed attention toward differences between them, differences so great as to be of kind rather than degree. Some CBC officials were furious, not because TV won, but because print lost.

The problem has been falsely seen as democracy *vs.* the mass media. But the mass media *are* democracy. The book itself was the first mechanical mass medium. What is really being asked, of course, is: can books' monopoly of knowledge survive the challenge of the new languages? The answer is: no. What should be asked is: what can print do better than any other medium and is that worth doing?

[7] From a personal communication to the author.

MEDIA LOG

Marshall McLuhan

About 1830 Lamartine pointed to the newspaper as the end of book culture: "The book arrives too late." At the same time Dickens used the press as base for a new impressionist art, which D. W. Griffiths and Sergei Eisenstein studied in 1920 as the foundation of movie art.

Robert Browning took the newspaper as art model for his impressionist epic *The Ring and the Book*; Mallarmé did the same in *Un Coup de Dés*.

Edgar Allan Poe, a newsman and, like Shelley, a science fictioneer, correctly analyzed the poetic process. Conditions of newspaper serial publication led both him and Dickens to the process of writing backward. This means simultaneity of all parts of a composition. Simultaneity compels sharp focus on *effect* of thing made. Simultaneity is the form of the press in dealing with Earth City. Simultaneity is formula for the writing of both detective story and symbolist poem. These are derivatives (one "low" and one "high") of the new technological culture. Simultaneity is related to telegraph, as the telegraph to math and physics.

Joyce's *Ulysses* completed the cycle of this technological art form.

The mass media are extensions of the mechanisms of human perception; they are imitators of the modes of human apprehension and judgment.

Technological culture in the newspaper form structures ordinary unawareness in patterns that correspond to the most sophisticated maneuvers of mathematical physics.

Newton's *Optics* created the techniques of picturesque and Romantic poetry.

The techniques of discontinuous juxtaposition in landscape poetry and painting were transferred to the popular press and the popular novel.

In 1830, due to this technological revolution, English popular consciousness was structured in ways that French and European intellectuals did not acquire until a later generation.

Average English and American unawareness has been ahead of official culture and awareness for two hundred years; therefore the English and American intellectual for two hundred years has automatically thrown in his lot with the average man against officialdom.

The Swiss cultural historian Giedion has had to invent the concept of "anonymous history" in order to write an account of the new technological culture in Anglo-Saxondom.

The professoriat has turned its back on culture for two hundred years because the high culture of technological society is popular culture and knows no boundaries between high and low.

The children of technological man respond with untaught delight to the poetry of trains, ships, planes, and to the beauty of machine products. In the schoolroom, officialdom suppresses all their natural experience; children are divorced from their culture. They are not permitted to approach the traditional heritage of mankind through the door of technological awareness; this only possible door for them is slammed in their faces. The only other door is that of the high-brow. Few find it, and fewer find their way back to popular culture.

T. S. Eliot has said he would prefer an illiterate audience, for the ways of official literacy do not equip the young to know themselves, the past, or the present. The technique of an Eliot poem is a direct application of the method of the popular radio-tube grid circuit to the shaping and control of the charge of meaning. An Eliot poem is one instance of a direct means of experiencing, under conditions of artistic control, the ordinary awareness and culture of contemporary man.

Photography and cinema have abolished realism as too easy; they substitute themselves for realism.

All the new media, including the press, are art forms that have the power of imposing, like poetry, their own assumptions. The new media are not ways of relating us to the old "real" world; they *are* the real world, and they reshape what remains of the old world at will.

Official culture still strives to force the new media to do the work of the old media. But the horseless carriage did not do the work of the horse; it abolished the horse and did what the horse could never do. Horses are fine. So are books.

Technological art takes the whole earth and its population as its material, not as its form.

It is too late to be frightened or disgusted, to greet the unseen with a sneer. Ordinary life-work demands that we harness and subordinate the media to human ends.

The media are not toys; they should not be in the hands of Mother Goose and Peter Pan executives. They can be entrusted only to new artists, because they are art forms.

Harnessing the Tennessee, Missouri, or Mississippi is kid stuff compared with curbing the movie, press, or television to human ends. The wild broncos of technological culture have yet to find their busters or masters. They have found only their P. T. Barnums.

Europeans cannot master these new powers of technology because they take themselves too seriously and too sentimentally. Europeans cannot imagine the Earth City. They have occupied old city spaces too long to be able to sense the new spaces created by the new media.

The English have lived longer with technological culture than anybody else, but they lost their chance to shape it when the ship yielded to the plane. But the English language is already the base of all technology.

The Russians are impotent to shape technological culture because of their inwardness and grimness. The future masters of technology will have to be lighthearted; the machine easily masters the grim.

Russian austerity is based on fear of the new media and their power to transform social existence. Russia stands pat on the status quo ante 1850 that produced Marx. There culture ends. The Russian revolution reached the stage of book culture.

Russian politicians have the same mentality as our professoriat: they wish technology would go away.

CHANNEL CAT IN THE MIDDLE DISTANCE

Jean Shepherd

Transcript of a recording, selected at random, of a disc jockey on WLW:

But here it is on a quiet February night   time to listen and time to sit, time to wait for the next channel cat to make the bend, time to wait for the next starfish to reproduce its kind, almost impossible to kill a starfish, you know, almost impossible even to understand a starfish. I once knew a starfish living just outside Hamilton, Ontario.

And if we cared to note we would see a tiny figure tattered and torn who seems to be having a few of the difficulties that he called upon himself   and a few extra, too   but then the machines were all well-oiled, you see   a few of them needed extra bearings   an occasional headgasket was there to be replaced, and a few of the valves needed grinding, too, but these things all in good time   all indeed in good time   it takes a little and it takes two.

Jean Shepherd: records, transcriptions   and it really does take that you know   it really takes that and a few things extra, too.

The whole thing is absolutely ridiculous as far as I'm concerned. This is the first time I've been ill   really the first time I've spent any time at all concerning myself with medicine   but nevertheless the business of being ill is an extremely interesting one   and for those who haven't tried it for some time, there are certain things you should pick up before you make a serious attempt to create a small one for yourself   getting back into business for yourself after you have been ill for awhile is much more interesting than being ill itself   to begin with, a large number of people didn't even know you were any place at all

disappointing   an extremely disappointing thing   I remember
seeing a cartoon   Charley Brown on telephone calling girlfriend
at party   saying he's ill and won't be able to come to the party
    girlfriend answering: that's O.K., didn't even know you weren't
here   Charley Brown hanging up telephone, looking quietly
into the middle distance   there are many things to be seen in
the middle distance   didn't even know you were gone   Monday night, yes, it's a Monday, sort of a Monday night   off into
the middle distance, strive and continue to strive, the three of
them, each one of whom has pulled the shortest straw of the
group.

And again its the golden touch   the inescapable, the always
present, the all-encompassing golden touch   a few years ago,
going out into left field, the old man made the mistake of allowing those in the dug-out   allowing them the brief luxury   the
realization   the knowledge   that he wasn't going to make it
you see, you've got to always give them the impression—you've
always got to keep it up   keep the footprints high, well up on
the front of the cushion   keep them moving.

Again the usage of the number 3   3A Sable Brush   future use,
future reference   card size itself is most important   the stories
and the scores upon scores of them that were told in the time
that passed were not necessarily stories of truth   nor were they
always stories   just a few words   an occasional period and
once in awhile a CAPITAL letter.

And while all the thoughts were being compiled and all the
words were being put down on 3 × 5 file cards   a few typewriter ribbons were being changed   and occasionally someone
took the time to oil the fielder's mitt   there were things to be
written, things to be said and things to be done   and there was
a quiet Monday night   a few people were listening   a few
people were looking   a few stars were being watched   a few
moons were being examined   a few sand dunes were being
understood as, in fact, had ever been understood in their brief
period of sitting before all the elders. It came to pass that the
writing was good   and we've been reading and we've been

looking   we've been cleaning windows, washing glasses and smoking cigarettes and from time to time changing typewriter ribbons. We have been clipping fingernails and we've been listening to recordings. We have been eating hamburgers and we've been eating auriomycin. We've been doing a thousand things and there have been one hundred moments that have passed and gone   some of them were good and most of them were forgotten   and that's the most important of all, I suppose   most of them were forgotten   just beginning things that passed. There seems to be too much smoke and it also seems the rugs are a little threadbare   the walls are not painted the right color and that's another one of the small troubles.

This is their way of going   their way of disappearing   and this is the thing students ten thousands years from now are really going to work upon   going to understand only vaguely and are going to make definite attempts to re-create   but these attempts are just exactly that   just attempts. I think this is going to be one of the wonderful things we have to offer above all things. This is probably a much recorded sentence   and when I speak of a sentence I mean a sentence in man's eternal struggle to create a chapter of himself rather than a paragraph, a line or perhaps a phrase   but this particular sentence   this particular sentence which could be called a century   this time   this period   has been recorded ten million ways   they've even recorded the disadvantages of keeping bananas in a refrigerator   they've recorded the advantages of liver stimulants of one kind or another   and the voices of presidents and cabinet ministers   they've also recorded the voices of little people speaking to one another on the street and there shall be a few of these conversations discovered, too   and it shall be the moment of discovery that will prove the small turning point in many a small scholar's career   this moment of discovery that was the way these people spoke   this is the way they talked and this is the way they sounded and really this is the way they were   and a small partial moon went scooting out over the curving river   it picked up speed and it picked up momentum and it picked up a few forgotten thoughts as it moved   a small partial moon   just a part   an example of life   an example of shadow   an example of creative thought   but it was just partial, you see   it wasn't complete   it never would be.

We have many nutcrackers to work with but no small picks which leads us exactly nowhere because that's exactly where we intended to be   there's no waiting and no wishing   step right up and 7 times over, 3 times down   there are 17 chairs, absolutely no waiting   everybody will be taken care of in time All Ice Cream Manufactured on the Premises.

It was a good, easy Monday night   the crowds were even more interesting than usual   but the old man was coasting more or less—coasting in between and in betwixt   what used to be called a liquid or even a solid in suspension, floating between the surface and the bottom   sort of in between   just floating in a colloidal suspension   I had difficulty with that one time and I was ready to surmount the difficulty and here we are floating again   and the surface glimmers and sheens   there's much to be said for surface tension, but that, too, will have to wait till after one o'clock when Grandma has put her knitting away and gone to bed. Yes, there will be a full field inspection at 0300.

JOYCE'S WAKE

W. R. Rodgers

Madame Leon: I had Gestapo visit us four times from different accusations and I never knew what they were going to accuse me of having done or whether it would end in an arrest of myself or **my husband.** Unfortunately, they picked my husband up between the third and their fourth visit, and one morning six months after my husband had been arrested and was being starved and frozen in one of the horror camps and I was frantically trying to help him, and establish some regular contact. I was terribly anxious. One morning I was dusting the books in my living room because even in moments of great emotional stress somehow you carry out every-day gestures, and there was a ring at the door. In fact, there were two long rings. I wondered who on earth that could be to see me in the morning so early, and I wasn't expecting any-one. I went to the door and there were two men both in civilian clothes. One wore a dark tweed suit and he turned up the lapel of his collar and he said: "Polizei Gestapo" and the second man was a Frenchman and he produced a card from the Vichy Min-ister with a red, white, and blue band across the corner, and I ushered them into the living room. And they came in and one of them sat down at the table. The same table where *Anna Livia* had been translated into French. And the Frenchman was prowl-ing around the room asking questions about various photographs on the wall. And suddenly the German asked me: "Who does your husband work for?" And I said he didn't work for anyone. And he said: "I know he worked for someone. We know it. You must tell us for whom he worked." And I kept denying this, and suddenly they pounced on the large portrait of Joyce we had, and they said, Who is this man? Is this your husband? I said, No, that was James Joyce, an Irish poet and writer. No, they said,

188

that was the man your husband worked for; where is he now? I said, He died, died in Zurich, didn't you know that? So they said, No, and then the German turned to me and said, That is why we have come. I said, Why? I didn't understand what he was driving at. So he said, Because we want first editions, and we think you must have some. So I said, Oh, why do you want first editions? So he answered, Because they have value.

Narrator: Paul Leon died at the hands of the Nazis. But before that, Joyce had reached Zurich. As Frau Giedion says:

Giedion: Joyce wanted only one thing: to find a place of peace where work and meditation were still possible. At last he found it. It was the 17th December, 1940, that he extricated himself from the confusions of war and reached Switzerland. "Here we still know where we stand," he said, as he looked around in a Swiss inn, shortly after his arrival.

Narrator: Penniless, homeless, and daughterless, he arrived, after long silence, exile, and cunning.

Giedion: Even thinner than usual he seemed, when we saw him getting off the train at Zurich, with his superior, rather mocking smile, which partly opened his thin lips, and half-astonished, half-absent eyes, which, magnified by glasses, seemed to live a life of their own. Immediately after first settling down, Joyce set off in search of a flat. I remember too he set out for the Librairie Francaise to find for his grandson a French edition of the Greek legends. You could see them walking in the snow, his hand in Stephen's, and the excited little boy pulling him forward, enchanted to see for the first time this white carpet, whilst Joyce, dazzled by the snow, seemed to suffer from the too blinding light. Then there was that last Christmas dinner that we shared with his family and himself. The songs, religious and secular, the Irish airs, the Latin canticles in which blended wonderfully the tenor voice of the father and the bass of his son Giorgio. Little Stephen demanded to sing under the table and the request was satisfied. James Joyce wanted to hear again the record he had bought some years earlier. It was "Ah Moon of My Delight," from Omar Rubaiyat Khayyam, sung by the Irish tenor John McCormack, whose voice, at its best, was so like that of Joyce himself.

I shall always remember that last invitation in the setting of an inn not far from the boarding house where he then lived. The walls of the low little room were wood paneled. Seated before a carafe of Fendant, Joyce delighted—dejected physically and mentally—in the astonishing climate of the Swiss stability. The whole setting of the inn gave an unusually comfortable intimacy. He gave a short résumé of the events and history of the last few months and emphasized the contrast between our peace, which he seemed to consider everlasting, and the storm outside. Nothing was more soothing for us than to hear this from a man accustomed to sounding the mysteries of the future. But the Swiss stability that enchanted him then did not hinder him from railing against the country and its proverbial cleanliness whose effect, according to him, was in some ways sterilizing. He even thrived upon this theme, and at the moment of goodbye he was talking enthusiastically on dirt. "You don't know how wonderful dirt is!" he exclaimed. We were then standing outside. The charming background of the old-fashioned inn, softly lit, was replaced by the cruel, cold black outside. His voice reached us in a murmur, through the dark. We said goodbye to him.

Narrator: It was January, 1941. There was a Renoir exhibition in Zurich. Joyce spent hours in front of it, fascinated, though semi-blind.

Giedion: On the 9th of January, accompanied by his old friend Paul Ruggiero, after a dinner with his favorite Neufchatel wine at an inn near the Lake, Joyce was overtaken by violent pain. He had been in a happy mood and rebelled humorously, as usual, against the strictly observed hour of closing. A neighboring doctor, called in the middle of the night, tried a too mild treatment. Forty-eight hours later an operation was decided upon. But it was too late. Joyce began to wander in delirium that evening and insisted again that Nora Joyce, who had not left him, should put her bed by the side of his. On the 13th of January at two o'clock in the morning death came without his having recovered consciousness. It was just the 13th, the date Joyce had always avoided for his journeys and for all decisions he had to make.

Narrator: That Joyce should have been taken ill on a Friday and have died on the 13th touched those who knew his feeling.

Giedion: I remember the burial, high up on a hill in Zurich, near the Zoo. A cold and wintry day hung over the wooded plain and the hillsides. A mysterious sun, milky and round like the moon, seemed to hide behind a misty glass.

Gasser: And it was a ghastly winter day with a lot of slush coming down from the sky, and there were no taxis any more, as the petrol rationing was very strict. I didn't—therefore I took a tram, and in this tram, going up the hill very slowly, there was assembled almost the whole funeral party. But they were all—the whole tram was, although I did not know many people, but they all talked about James Joyce. It was Lord and Lady Derwent, who was cultural attaché at the British Legation in Berne during the war, and it was his eye-doctor, and the secretary of Paul Klee, the painter, as far as I remember, as it is rather a long time since. We arrived at the cemetery, and were directed into a chapel, but as James Joyce did not want to have a priest at his funeral, there was nobody there, and the attendants of the mortician—they were rather—it was very strange to them, because they did not know what to do, as usually in Switzerland one has priest, either Catholic or a Protestant.

The main speech was given by Lord Derwent, who was usually very brusque, but, I think, as he had to perform an official duty, he performed a rather formal funeral speech. And after this we went out into the snow again, and the coffin was carried in front of us, and we walked right to the end of the wall, where the hole for the grave was dug. Meanwhile, in the distance there was the faint roar of the wild animals in the zoo, and we stood round the grave, and again didn't quite know what to do, because again there was no priest, and this time not even an official funeral speech. So we hoaxed each other in a very embarrassed way until a very, very old man turned up—obviously a man who hovers over the grave, as one sees in almost every churchyard, men who seem to just wait till they are buried themselves. A tiny man who obviously was deaf, because he went to one of those attendants of the mortician, who was holding the rope that went under the coffin, as the coffin was not sunk yet into the grave, and he asked, "Who is buried here?" And the mortician said, "Mr. Joyce." And again in front of the whole assemblance of mourners he seemed not to have understood it. He again asked, "Who is it?" "Mr. Joyce," he shouted, and at that moment, the coffin was lowered into the grave.

Narrator: James Joyce had accomplished his destiny. He had flown past the nets.

Eva Joyce: His last words struck me forcibly as the keynote of his whole life. His last words were that he thought, "Does nobody understand?"—and I'm afraid that's what none of us did—understand him. . . .

Quinlan: But when you sum the whole thing up, you see, and mind you it is important because after all when you've read all a man has written, you see, and you ask yourself the final question—you will want to know what exactly was deep down in his mind. To me anyway, this is serious, to be personal—I may be completely unfounded—however, I think that if you observe that peculiar detachment the man had, in all his personal relations, and the objective, sort of remote treatment of the themes of sex, nationality—almost everything in fact—I think you can only explain that sort of personality by the fact that deep in his nature there was an incessant and a morbid preoccupation with conscience—a despair, a theological despair, as we call it—which he kept at bay by untiring devotion to work and by that inordinate artistic ambition. You remember that vocation which he chose for himself—the artifex and so on, you see—the uncreated conscience.

Well, the thing I'd like to know most of all is this: what was in the mind of Joyce when he wasn't writing—when he wasn't playing host to his powers—what was in his mind in his most desolate hour? And, most of all, what was in his mind in his last conscious moments, when the ego faltered? I, in charity, and indeed in sympathy, want to believe this: that beneath the lather of his art, of his life, of the poverty of Trieste, Paris, and Zurich, and of this pain—I want to believe that he saw again the very City of God.

Eva Joyce: There is, I hope, somebody that did understand him who was able to answer that question, and I believe that it was answered. But my fervent belief is that he's all right. I hope to God he is. But I don't see why he wouldn't be because what harm did he to anybody?

Well, my personal idea about his life was that it was a tragedy because he was misunderstood; he had a lovely character, he had a lovely outlook on life. But he was—I don't know why he was in a sense a failure which, I suppose, he appeared to be and seemed to think he was himself, I could never understand, because he was a genius, he was gentle, he could have put his brain to anything. And the writings—I don't like to discuss his writings because, well, I'm only talking about him as my own brother and as I met him as an ordinary individual member of the family. I must say the tragedy of his life which prompted him to write as he wrote, that's always what puzzled me and there must have been something—he was reacting in his writings—something that —an over-wrought process—something that had nettled him, or he was giving vent to it in his writings—well, I can't explain, it was—that wasn't Jim—when he was writing it wasn't Jim, as I knew him and as we all knew him. He was just a lovable individual; and he was a gentle father, he was a kind brother, he was a lovable son and he was kind to everybody that he came in contact with—such tremendous kindness.

Stanislaus Joyce: I confess I have no better explanation to offer of his triumphant struggle to preserve his rectitude as an artist in the midst of illness and disappointment, in abject poverty and disillusionment, than this, that he who has loved God intensely in youth will never love anything less. The definition may change, the service abides.

James Joyce:

well you know

or don't you kennet

or haven't I told you

every

TELLING

ⱢⱯIⱢIИG

TAILING

has a   and

that's

the   of

HE   and the She

—  LOOK

look

the

DUSK

is GROWING

LOFTY

my branches LOFTY are taking R
O
O
T

and my 

ashley

COMMUNICATIONS REVOLUTION

Gilbert Seldes

Before print, communication was by voice and manuscript; both imposed limitations. At best a speaker addressed a few hundred at a time, the writer only those to whom a letter or scroll could be circulated. With print came communication that could be endlessly duplicated.

Print made illiterates inferior, gave rise to a new discipline: learning to read. Changes that followed were marked in virtually every aspect of life; resistance to them was as common as resistance now is to changes electronics are bringing about.

One of the commonest criticisms is that movies, radio, TV can't substitute for textbooks. Centuries ago printed books for students were denounced because they couldn't have the authority of teachers speaking directly to students. So, in past and present, a common effect: any institution that lasts a long time creates vested interests, and people who benefit by it are inclined to protect the institution as a way of protecting themselves.

Print	*Electronics*
1. Requires ability to read	1. No special training required
2. Usually experienced individually	2. Usually experienced in company
3. Taken in small doses	3. Taken in large doses
4. Relatively slow diffusion	4. Very rapid diffusion
5. Can be reread and checked	5. Generally not available for re-observation
6. Relatively inexpensive to produce but costly to the consumer	6. Very expensive to produce but relatively cheap for the consumer
7. Created for minorities of varying sizes	7. Created for majorities

The high-speed press and later processes made print cheap; parallel developments in transportation made diffusion easy. The availability of print made education (in print at least) more desirable; at the same time print was the major tool of instruction in virtually all branches of schooling. In the U.S., growing population, increased wealth, leisure, created a vast public for printed matter. But technology also created illustrations (halftone photograph, colored comics, etc.) providing a kind of print that required less reading. The popularity of illustrations opened the way for the large-circulation magazines—*Life, Look*—which use visual effects to attract readers to reading matter of a relatively high intellectual order.

If print made it possible to establish in the U.S. a nation whose political life was based on public opinion, as Marshall McLuhan says, do the electronic successors of print tend to nullify and manipulate, rather than inform, public opinion? If this is the case, the tabloid and comic tend in the same direction, whereas the thoughtful mass-magazine is a counter-weight on the side of the older book culture. The lavish use of illustration arrived at a high point after the movie but before TV, as if to give print a chance to attract people whose eyes would be constantly caught by the visual image.

Movies took the place of the theatre rather than of print, though time spent at them might have been spent in reading. They brought to millions, who were not habitual readers, novels, old and new, biographies, history. They came to vast numbers never reached by the theatre, made entertainment more accessible, far less costly. But people still had to leave their homes for it, pay for it; entertainment was still "a sometimes thing," a reward for children, even for adults who had saved up the price and arranged free time. Entertainment remained set apart from daily life. Radio and TV integrated it into the daily routine.

Radio was the pivot on which the communications revolution turned. For the first time in modern history, entertainment, news, ideas, entered the home to accompany household tasks; their integration into daily life was emphasized by placing entertainment in the context of news on one side, advertisements on the other. Within a short time, radio became a necessity; being a necessity it couldn't be a reward. We all began to feel we had a right to the entertainment radio provided.

On the day *Childe Harold's* pilgrimage was published (1811), "I woke," said Lord Byron, "and found myself famous." The morning after the release of his first picture, the dog called "Lassie" was famous. Fame in Byron's time meant being spoken of by perhaps 2000 people who read *Childe Harold* in the year after publication; fame for Lassie meant adoration on the part of ten million. Probably every literate person heard of Byron, just as everyone, including non-moviegoers, heard of Lassie, but illiteracy in England in 1811 may have been 90 per cent; there's no "illiteracy" in films.

As the number of addressed increases, subject and style alter. We know this to be true in the simplest of our relationships. We relate incidents differently to our family, to a group of acquaintances, or to a public meeting. Whole areas of discourse aren't suited to universal communication. The closely knit argument of an expert legislator can't be followed at a banquet; the statesman turns demagogue with a microphone, not out of corruption of character, but because he has to adapt his style, even if he doesn't change his objective, to the medium that carries his voice and the circumstances in which his voice is heard. A sense of the appropriate also operates: an expert broadcasting on financial matters, unless he is being intentionally jocose, won't say a project will cost $169,875,912.84; he will use round figures lest a home listener retains only the eighty-four cents.

In 1934 William S. Paley, head of CBS, told his associates that he would like them to arrange to broadcast the Sunday afternoon programs of the New York Philharmonic. Told there was no audience for classical music, he replied, "If there isn't, we'll create it."

It's probable that in 1934 the number of regular listeners to symphonic music was in the order of 100,000. Ten years later, when the Philharmonic Concerts became a sponsored program, it was perhaps 10,000,000. The devotion of this audience was demonstrated when, a few years later, the network ceased broadcasting the Philharmonic directly from Carnegie Hall and used instead a recording. Protests were so numerous and intense, the original schedule had to be restored. A cohesive audience had been brought into being.

"An Englishman," said Shaw, "thinks he is being moral when he is only uncomfortable." We hear a sermon on the good life and we see a movie in which the hero has a good time—no one can say with certainty which has the greater influence on our lives. Eliot writes, "It is just the literature that we read for 'amusement' or 'purely for pleasure' that may have the greatest and least suspected influence on us. And it is chiefly contemporary literature that the majority of people ever read in this attitude of 'purely for pleasure.' Though we may read literature merely for pleasure, or 'entertainment' or 'esthetic enjoyment', this reading affects us as entire human beings; it affects our moral and religious existence."

THE SOVIET PRESS

Arthur Gibson

In the United States and England it is the freedom of expression, the right itself in the abstract, that is valued. . . .
In the Soviet Union, on the other hand, the *results* of exer-
cising freedom are in the forefront of attention, and preoccupation with the freedom itself is secondary. It is for this
reason that discussions between Soviet and Anglo-American
representatives characteristically reach absolutely no agreement on specific proposals, although both sides assert that
there should be freedom of the press. The American is usually talking about freedom of *expression,* the *right* to say or
not to say certain things, a right which he claims exists in
the United States and not in the Soviet Union. The Soviet
representative is usually talking about *access* to the *means* of
expression, not to the right to say things at all, and this access
he maintains is denied to most in the United States and exists
for most in the Soviet Union.[1]

Alex Inkeles

Soviet concern with media *results,* rather than media *contents,* is identical with the outlook of our advertising enterprises,
where the idea of self-expression would never arise. Indeed the
function of the entire Soviet press is similar to our ads in shaping
production and social processes.

Basic to any approach to the Soviet press is study of those
areas of getting the newspaper before the book. The press was
the first extensive awareness for them of our print technology.
We had had the book for centuries before we felt the results of
the press revolution. The book isolates the reader and not only
builds up an intense commodity consciousness via this transport-

[1] *Public Opinion in Russia,* Cambridge, Mass., Harvard University
Press, 1950, p. 137.

able and private article but also promotes a close person-to-person relation between author and reader, which is almost wholly absent in the press.

The press page speaks as many to many, not as person-to-person. After centuries of book habitude, the press merely intensified our personal interests. Our press inevitably discovered "human interest" because in a person-to-person book culture that was the main audience attitude with which it had to work.

Europeans in general never felt the result of book culture in any degree approaching its development in the English-speaking world. The greater diversity of cultural interests in Europe in the 16th century reduced the effect of the book on them, just as our greater degree of book culture diminished the emotional results of the newspaper among us as compared with the Soviet area. The European could on the other hand use the daily paper as a high-brow form of expression and the movie likewise, whereas our predisposition was to treat both as mere vulgarizations of the book. The Soviet and Europe alike could take the press seriously as a daily collective educator, whereas for us the very collective character of the press as many speaking simultaneously to many conflicted with our bias toward the book as educator in the form of one writer speaking to one reader.

Not committed exclusively to the book form, the European has never felt the same interest in the "human interest" story or the private point of view in news reporting. Certainly in the Soviet there is strong bias against the individual story and the private expression of opinion. And this has little to do with Communism or Marxism. The collective form of the press encountered there a culture that was still feudally socialized and collective. The collective form of the press, which in our book culture intensified individualism, there intensified socialism. What we consider "objective" news, they consider the uninteresting voice of a private individual. Much more interesting and reliable in their eyes or ears is the voice of an agency of the state. Again, this attitude predated Marxism by decades and extends beyond the Soviet bloc.

The U.S.A. is the extreme instance of book culture. It got this latest form of European technology and very little else from

Europe in the 17th century. There was nothing in America to modify the impact of print technology. This first form of mechanization of a handicraft got an intensity of stress in our lives unlike any other area before or since. Individualist in its social and personal results, collectivist in its assembly-line means of production, the book has saddled us with that strange paradox that prompts us to pursue revolutionary industrial changes while still insisting upon business as usual.

The format of any Soviet newspaper is completely different from that of any North American one. Selecting one typical "capital" paper, *Pravda,* and one typical provincial one, *Zarya Vostoka,* these differences can be traced thus:

There is a complete absence in Soviet papers of commercial advertising. The lower right-hand corner of the last page of both papers comes closest to it. In *Pravda* this corner carries a drab, factual account, of no more than 3 lines, of what is being offered "Today in Moscow Theatres." *Zarya Vostoka* prints in this corner the occasional death notice, the more than occasional notifications of applications for divorce, the odd notice of a local football game. But of the insistent, competitive advertising of American papers, there's not a trace. How could there be since there are no competing businesses? Everybody knows that the things he needs can be obtained in either the gigantic cooperatives or the black market.

Under the masthead of *Pravda* it says, "Organ of Central Committee of Communist Party of USSR"; under *Zarya Vostoka,* "Organ of Central and Tiflis Committees of Communist Party of Georgia and of the Soviet of Workers' Deputies of the Georgian SSR." Every paper is a mouth-piece of a central or regional government committee. Competition between privately owned papers and, a fortiori, between those of differing political allegiance is impossible.

Sensationalism, the desire to catch the eye with the headline, to cram more into it than is contained in the article itself, is utterly absent. Headlines never reach a height of more than one-quarter of an inch. Varying types accent importance, but the general impression is one of shabby gentility. Action verbs are unknown. Not only is the headline non-sensational; it's deliberately uninformative—either a simple announcement of the nature of the article, or an ecstatic socio-political slogan. Here are random examples of major page 1 headlines from nonfestive issues of *Pravda* and *Zarya Vostoka:*

Arrival of Burmese Prime Minister U Nu in Moscow

Declaration of Soviet Government to Government of Iran Letter of President of Soviet of Ministers of Soviet Union, N. A. Bulganin, to President of the U.S.A., Dwight D. Eisenhower

Presentation of Credentials to President of Presidium of Supreme Soviet of USSR, K. E. Voroshilov, by the Ambassador Extraordinary and Plenipotentiary of the Federated People's Republic of Yugoslavia, Velko Mitchunovitch

Exchange of Messages between President of Presidium of Supreme Soviet of USSR, K. E. Voroshilov and President of Islamic Republic of Pakistan, Iskander Mira

On festive occasions both carry on page 1 in quarter-inch type, lighter than that of the main headlines, some message, which recurs, year after year, on the same feast:

Under the Banner of World-transforming Doctrine of Marxism-Leninism, the Communist Party of the Soviet Union Will Lead the Soviet People to the Complete Victory of Communism
    (From the speech of the 1st Secretary of Central Committee of Communist Party of USSR, Comrade N. S. Khrushchev)

Workers of the Soviet Union! Let Us Rally Still More Closely Round the Communist Party and the Soviet Government, Let Us Mobilize All Our Forces and Creative Energy for the Great Task of the Establishment of Communist Society!
    (From the Proclamation of the Central Committee of the Communist Party of the Soviet Union, on the 38th Anniversary of the Great October Socialist Revolution)

On nonfestive days this space is taken up by a sort of table of contents, which is always in small type and as uninformative as the headlines. It abounds in "Concerning the question of . . . ," "About . . . ," "On . . . ," and in factual statements of subjects of articles, which statements usually contain no verbs.

On festive days the entire first page is usually taken up by some Appeal, Proclamation, Message, or Resolution, e.g.:

> Proclamation of Central Committee of Communist Party on 38th Anniversary of Great October Socialist Revolution

On nonfestive days, the left quarter of page 1 in both papers is devoted to editorial comment. This always deals with some matter of immediate interest, is almost always unsigned, and is strictly party line in vocabulary, turn of phrase, and general outlook:

> Prepare School-children for Practical Activity
>
> Great Irresistible Force of Soviet Patriotism
>
> Decisive Days in Harvesting and Preserving Vegetables
>
> New Stage in Development of Relations between USSR and German Federal Republic

Individual exploits, joys, sorrows, heroism, and crimes of this or that person get no space. There are no crime stories as such, no sensational disclosures, complimentary or otherwise, about private lives. What is central is the collective, unremitting effort to build Communist society. Newspapers report faithfully and verbatim Directives of the Party and speeches of its leaders. Each speech is accompanied by a mug-shot, that is, a full-face, backgroundless photograph of the speaker. One entire number of *Pravda* (an unusually large one of 9 pages) was devoted exclusively to verbatim reporting of speeches at the 20th Congress of the Party, except for one quarter-page World News and Theatre Information. The papers then editorialize round these directives. They report the Awards of Order of Lenin to factories or cities (rarely to individuals) that have distinguished themselves, usually by surpassing production quotas set by the Government. Their coverage of world news is extremely selective and concerned with what other people think of the Soviet experiment (they invariably think well of it), what is being said in favor of Communism in other countries, what is being said against Communism's enemies, and world weather if newsworthy. News need not be new. Articles often deal with events of months before, announced now for the first time. Recently *Pravda* has provided space for letters to the editor "containing complaints and suggestions for improvements in working and living conditions."

The prose of all papers is astonishingly similar. Long sentences, perpetual repetition, and scrupulous grammaticality (even the humblest worker quoted speaks impeccable Russian party-line prose) produce a strangely soporific effect. Day after day, it pours forth from every column of every paper, e.g.:

> *Pravda,* on the 38th Anniversary of the Revolution: "The history of humanity has never known such a wise and unshakable leader of the masses as is our great Communist Party, founded and trained by the immortal Lenin. Under the leadership of the Party, our people attained the world-famed, historic victory in October, 1917, resisted all attacks on the October Revolution by each and every foe, established Socialism and now goes confidently forward to Communism."

> *Pravda,* October 6: "There is no doubt that the Soviet technological intelligentsia, true to its patriotic duty, will bend all its forces to the successful solution of the great problems set Socialist industry by the Communist Party and the Soviet Government, that it will bring a worthy contribution to the task of further strengthening the economic might of the homeland, to the task of the establishment of Communism."

There's not a single editorial in *Pravda*'s history that doesn't deal with some feature of the establishment of Communism. A typical page of *Pravda* or *Zarya Vostoka* will suffice to show how "monolithic" this interest is:

> *Pravda,* September 8: Masthead with wreath-encircled Lenin head and slogan "Proletarians of all lands, unite!"; editorial on Normalization of Relations between USSR and German Federal Republic; news items: Kolkhozi and Sovkhozi, which have fulfilled ahead of time the Government quota for bread production; presentation of credentials of Netherlands' Ambassador; 280,000 young Mechanical Specialists; "Our place—in the Kolkhoz" (Cooperative Farm); Soldiers Guests of Magnitogorsk Metalurgists; Rich Vegetable Harvest in Sakhalin; Industrial Exhibition in Minsk.

> *Zarya Vostoka,* April 5: an article by a Master in a Shoe Factory berating those who try to learn their trade far

from the actual factories. Comrade Kavtaradze begins by quoting Comrade Khrushchev; a contribution by one Bardushvili on the urgent tasks of the coal industry in Georgia; notes on the arrival in England of the Lalenkov delegation, in Yugoslavia of a delegation of USSR "Parliamentarians," and in Haiphong of two Soviet ships.

Day in, day out, page 1 or page 4, nothing but one concentrated, monolithic, soporific advertisement for Communist society. If an article is written on the centenary of Heine it's to prove he is "one of the noblest of creative writers, a fighter for a better future for humanity."

FIVE SOVEREIGN FINGERS TAXED THE BREATH

Marshall McLuhan

The CITY no longer exists, except as a cultural ghost for tourists. Any highway eatery with its TV set, newspaper, and magazine is as cosmopolitan as New York or Paris.

The PEASANT was always a suburban parasite. The farmer no longer exists; today he is a "city" man.

The METROPOLIS today is a classroom; the ads are its teachers. The classroom is an obsolete detention home, a feudal dungeon.

The metropolis is OBSOLETE. Ask the Army.

The INSTANTANEOUS global coverage of radio-tv makes the city form meaningless, functionless. Cities were once related to the realities of production and intercommunication. Not now.

Until WRITING was invented, we lived in acoustic space, where the Eskimo now lives: boundless, directionless, horizonless, the dark of the mind, the world of emotion, primordial intuition, terror. Speech is a social chart of this dark bog.

SPEECH structures the abyss of mental and acoustic space, shrouding the race; it is a cosmic, invisible architecture of the human dark. Speak that I may see you.

WRITING turned a spotlight on the high, dim Sierras of speech; writing was the visualization of acoustic space. It lit up the dark.

These five kings did a king to death.

A goose's quill put an end to talk, abolished mystery, gave architecture and towns, brought roads and armies, bureaucracies. It was the basic metaphor with which the cycle of CIVILIZATION began, the step from the dark into the light of the mind. The hand that filled a paper built a city.

The handwriting is on the celluloid walls of Hollywood; the

Age of Writing has passed. We must invent a NEW META-PHOR, restructure our thoughts and feelings. The new media are not bridges between man and nature: they are nature.

The MECHANIZATION of writing mechanized the visual-acoustic metaphor on which all civilization rests; it created the classroom and mass education, the modern press and telegraph. It was the original assembly line.

Gutenberg made all history SIMULTANEOUS: the transportable book brought the world of the dead into the space of the gentleman's library; the telegraph brought the entire world of the living to the workman's breakfast table.

PHOTOGRAPHY was the mechanization of the perspective painting and of the arrested eye; it broke the barriers of the nationalist, vernacular space created by printing. Printing upset the balance of oral and written speech; photography upset the balance of ear and eye.

Telephone, gramophone, and RADIO are the mechanization of postliterate acoustic space. Radio returns us to the dark of the mind, to the invasions from Mars and Orson Welles; it mechanizes the well of loneliness that is acoustic space: the human heart-throb put on a PA system provides a well of loneliness in which anyone can drown.

Movies and TV complete the cycle of mechanization of the human sensorium. With the omnipresent ear and the moving eye, we have abolished writing, the specialized acoustic-visual metaphor that established the dynamics of Western civilization.

By surpassing writing, we have regained our WHOLENESS, not on a national or cultural, but cosmic, plane. We have evoked a super-civilized sub-primitive man.

NOBODY yet knows the language inherent in the new technological culture; we are all deaf-blind mutes in terms of the new situation. Our most impressive words and thoughts betray us by referring to the previously existent, not to the present.

We are back in acoustic space. We begin again to structure the primordial feelings and emotions from which 3000 years of literacy divorced us.

Hands have no tears to flow.